MW00639786

THE CRISIS OF CULTURE

OLIVIER ROY

The Crisis of Culture

Identity Politics and the Empire of Norms

Translated by
Cynthia Schoch and Trista Selous

OXFORD
UNIVERSITY PRESS

OXFORD
UNIVERSITY PRESS

Oxford University Press is a department of the
University of Oxford. It furthers the University's objective
of excellence in research, scholarship, and education
by publishing worldwide.

Oxford   New York

Auckland   Cape Town   Dar es Salaam   Hong Kong   Karachi
Kuala Lumpur   Madrid   Melbourne   Mexico City   Nairobi
New Delhi   Shanghai   Taipei   Toronto

With offices in

Argentina   Austria   Brazil   Chile   Czech Republic   France   Greece
Guatemala   Hungary   Italy   Japan   Poland   Portugal   Singapore
South Korea   Switzerland   Thailand   Turkey   Ukraine   Vietnam

Oxford is a registered trade mark of Oxford University Press
in the UK and certain other countries.

Published in the United States of America by
Oxford University Press
198 Madison Avenue, New York, NY 10016

Library of Congress Cataloging-in-Publication Data is available
Olivier Roy.
The Crisis of Culture: Identity Politics and the Empire of Norms.
ISBN: 9780197782514

Printed in the United Kingdom on acid-free paper
by Bell and Bain Ltd, Glasgow

CONTENTS

INTRODUCTION

On 27 January 2018 United Airlines refused to allow a passenger onto an aeroplane with a peacock, even though the passenger had a medical certificate stating that the presence of the bird was vital to enable her to bear the mental stress of flying. In a press release, the airline said that the peacock's presence in the cabin "did not meet the guidelines for a number of reasons, including its weight and size".[1] In the same period the same scene was played out in several airports with other creatures, including a pit-bull, a squirrel, a pig, a duck, a marmoset, a turkey and a miniature horse. The passengers involved all demanded to have the creature in the cabin with them as "emotional support" and often had a medical certificate to that effect. After a while, American airline companies decided to establish new guidelines stating which pets were acceptable (a kitten in a basket) and which were not (an alligator, whether or not on a lead).

Anecdotes of this kind raise questions, though I have deliberately chosen an example that elicits more smiles than arguments (we will consider other, more controversial cases later). Of what are such stories a symptom? How should they be classified if not under "other news"? They are not sufficiently common to be regarded as a social trend, they do not launch social or political movements, and their protagonists alone must face the disapproval aroused by their actions. Yet in the case above they had a real effect: the writing of new guidelines. For, as the press release notes, there are "a number of reasons" not to allow a peacock to travel in the cabin of an aeroplane, and these must be spelled out. A person can ask for their distress to be considered and, once off the plane, can go to court to demand compensation, even though that distress—which pre-existed the incident and had now become trauma—is not caused by any deliberate action by a third party. The court is given the task of validating or invalidating the demand and, in the case of validation, to set the level of damages—in other words to quantify distress and set a public value on a private emotion. An insignificant event suddenly takes on extreme proportions.

Why were new guidelines needed? Because things that had seemed obvious, at least within the same culture, are suddenly no longer so. Twenty or thirty years ago it might have seemed absurd, fantastical or even insane to get on a plane with a peacock. The case would not have gone before a court—or only to be tried as a public order offence. The fact that in 2018 the airline responded by referring to "a number of reasons", rather than a simple "no", indicates that there were new issues here, two of which are immediately apparent: the place of animals (in allocated seats and the order of living things)—which questions the place of human beings by comparison—and the passenger's distress, which could not be simply disregarded without the risk of being sued. The airline's "other reasons" require nothing short of an update to the classification of animals, as made in the days of the Book of Genesis, when God left it to Adam to do the job (once and for all as He no doubt assumed), on condition that he remained in his own place (which he failed to do and relates to this book). What was once regarded as the settled line between humans and animals is now being challenged. A human in distress needs an animal for comfort and thereby removes the difference between a tame animal or pet and a wild animal. All animals have become pets because the place of human beings has become decentred. These are the days of veganism and antispeciesism. Animals have been recognised as "suffering" or, more precisely, as "sentient". Categories that once enabled the drawing of distinctions (mechanism and instinct for animals, soul, mind and reason for human beings) have given way to shared feelings of sensitivity and suffering. Suffering opens up the issue of rights—the right not to suffer—and thus norms—the prevention or remediation of suffering. This in turn means that culturally accepted premises must be changed so that we can rethink our relationship with animals, in terms of food (veganism), leisure activities (bans on hunting, fishing and bull-fighting), the law (who represents animals, if they are legal subjects but incapable of acting for themselves?) and even humanitarian priorities (the kennels authorised by British Prime Minister Boris Johnson to be evacuated from Kabul in late August 2021, rather than the fleeing men, women and children). If we can no longer place human beings between animals and angels, if we swap that vertical axis for one that is horizontal, in other words flat and stretched by the infinitesimal reduction of small differences, humanism is in crisis. And there's nothing so odd in that. From Marx to Derrida via Nietzsche and Freud, "the philosophy of suspicion" was always a critique of humanism, so it should come as no surprise that animals come into the minds of decentred human beings. But this book is not about animals, it is about culture. Animals simply embody the difficulties we have in thinking about nature, and thus also about culture.

Why is nature making a comeback in our imaginary? Because nothing is culturally self-evident anymore, we can no longer take anything for granted. Although Western thought always contrasted culture with nature (and this is true of both Greek philosophy and Christianity), the current debate around nature is a consequence of the crisis of culture.

But if things can no longer be taken for granted, what about right and wrong, good and evil? How can we conceptualise values if things are no longer culturally self-evident?

Something has happened.

Our ideas of good and evil have changed considerably in the last thirty years. Or rather (since there have always been progressives, conservatives, idealists, cynics and assorted radicals), what has changed is the space in which good and evil are configured. This has not (or not necessarily) been brought about by a new generation, still less by a revolution, a power grab, the emergence of a new religion (even if the domain of spirituality has emptied while simultaneously filling up) or an epidemic (we cannot blame Covid-19 for everything). Why have one cohort of people—and my generation of baby boomers has been well-placed both to understand and experience this—changed their core values over the course of fifty years, when nothing obliged them to do so? Why have their children and grandchildren become so detached from the cultural references of their elders?[2]

Looking back, we see that what once seemed obvious, progressive and thus desirable, is now seen as unacceptable and, crucially, unthinkable, for example sexual freedom leading to new forms of sexual harassment. Why has the great utopia of 1960s liberation led to an expansion of systems of moral and legal normativity, in the absence of any call to order?[3]

Let us take an example. I should start by stating that I intend no criticism of the person cited, in this case *New York Times* columnist Maureen Dowd. We are of the same generation and I could doubtless have been subject to the same criticism had I written a little too much. Everyone has the right to change their mind, to become a convert and reject their past. I very much liked the film *Blow Up*, which was considered avant-garde in its day and might now be seen as an apology for rape. I liked Coluche and Desproges, who would undoubtedly be heavily criticised today (Coluche: "God created alcohol so that ugly women still get to fuck").[4]

Maureen Dowd has been writing columns for the *New York Times* since 1983. In two of her pieces for that paper, written twenty years apart, she comments on the Monica Lewinsky affair, in which a young intern at the White House was drawn into a sexual relationship with President Bill Clinton. This is what Dowd wrote in 1999 (supplementing the Lewinsky story with that of Joyce Maynard, who had just published a book on her relationship with novelist J. D. Salinger, thirty-four years her senior). The article is entitled "Liberties; Leech Women in Love!":

> Throughout the long, dark ages of undisputed patriarchy, women connived to trade beauty and sex for affluence and status.... These two highly skilled predators keep trying to extract celebrity from old love affairs that were not only brief and puerile but sexually tortured. They want to gain immortality—and big bucks—by feeding off the detritus of their triste trysts with older, famous men.[5]

Harsh!

And here is Dowd in 2018, writing again about Lewinsky, who has just written a book about her relationship with the older man, as Maynard had done before her:

> The power differential between a 22-year-old intern and a 49-year-old boss makes any sexual interaction wrong. And if you throw in the fact that he was President—the country's parent and someone serving in loco parentis for the youngest White House staffers—it's an inexcusable abuse of power ... As [Lewinsky] wrote in an eloquent March *Vanity Fair* piece, "I'm beginning to entertain the notion that in such a circumstance the idea of consent might well be rendered moot".[6]

How do you go from "leech" to victim in twenty years, when no new element has emerged?

Dowd is clearly sincere in both articles; she has not been forced to change her mind; instead she has simply changed her points of reference.

It is this paradigm shift that interests me here. Are we living in a new culture or, conversely, is this expansion of normativity the sign of a profound crisis in the notion of culture itself? That is the question I pose.

1

THE CRISIS IN QUESTION

From feminism and the crisis of masculinity to racism and intersectionality, gender versus biological sex, identity versus universalism, cultural appropriation, "wokeism", cancel culture, "dumbing down", censorship and the purging of artworks and literary classics—not to mention immigration—today's political conflicts are focused more on values and identity than on the economy and specifically social questions.

Central to all these debates is the issue of culture—taken in all the meanings of the word—the literary and artistic canon (high culture) and the anthropological construction specific either to a society or a community within the dominant society. At stake are the very codes and symbols that comprise social ties, and which are encapsulated rigidly in discussions about identity.

Another point in common is a ferocious polarisation, manifested in curses, threats, denunciations, fake news, censorship, and so on. All this has led to the ever-increasing moral and judicial indictment of social relations. Beyond a debate of ideas, there is an attempt not only to impose new norms, but to extend the very domain of normativity (to sexual intimacy, for instance).

How is it that Western societies that claim to be liberal—the remarkable extension of the domain of political, sexual, economic and artistic freedom over a half-century—have brought about an equally remarkable extension of the realm of norms? Thus, we have witnessed the judicialisation of everyday life as well as the normative scrutiny of different domains and an increased appeal to pedagogical authority to impose new norms, whether pertaining to secularism, sexuality or religious practices.

Beneath harsh words, there is nevertheless general agreement as to the description of the crisis, if not an analysis of it. Everyone can identify forces dividing society, even if we argue over how to interpret them, in other words over the values being promoted or rejected. Every statement is a value judgement, even by those who have the illusion of being "axiologically neutral."

There is a consensus that we are in a conflict over cultural models. People lock horns over the "values" embodied by these antagonistic cultural models (religious versus hedonistic values, "Western" versus Islamic values, particular identities versus human rights, etc.). Conservatives denounce challenges to the notion of family and sexual division; feminists want to end all forms of patriarchal culture (such as "rape culture"). Others hunt down "cancel culture" on college campuses or discuss the clash of cultures (renamed the "clash of civilisations"). There is much handwringing over "cultural insecurity." Debates rage over republican, secular, religious and national "values." Culture is undoubtedly at the centre of preoccupations, even if the meaning of the word itself remains vague, as it does for "cultivated." There seems to be agreement that an information technology revolution has occurred and has spawned an "internet culture," which in turn has altered social ties, the relationship to knowledge and communication in general. We also know that other digital and scientific advances (genetics, artificial intelligence) are changing our relationship to life itself and consequently altering the relationship between nature and culture, which in turn shapes the fight against climate change and begs the question: should the traditional subjugation of nature to culture (in every sense of the term) be reversed? Moreover, the expansion of a global neoliberal economy clearly jeopardises societies that have formed in the shadow of nation states. Lastly, everyone is attuned to what globalisation implies in terms of mobility, migration, hybridisation, shifting relations between minorities and majorities, and the disappearance of physical borders that people try to re-erect and reactivate in the imaginary register of identity.

From freedom to normativity

So what is the crisis all about? Roughly, four levels of radical transformation have changed the world since the 1960s: 1) the transformation of values with the individualist and hedonist revolution of the 1960s; 2) the internet revolution; 3) neoliberal financial globalisation; 4) the globalisation of space and the movement of human beings, in other words deterritorialisation.

Countless scholarly works, remarkable essays and even some novels have attempted to connect all these areas, to delve more deeply into certain aspects and identify new horizons. Francis Fukuyama and Samuel Huntington were among the first; Michel Houellebecq, Jean-Claude Michéa and more recently Christophe Guilluy in France; and on the political left, David Graeber, Eva Illouz and Béatrice Hibou. These authors will be quoted extensively here, but my aim is not to undertake another thorough survey of the question.

My book seeks to analyse the relationships between those four levels from two different angles: culture and norms. Are we simply living through a transition between two cultural models, one liberal/internet/cosmopolitan/feminist, the other traditional/conservative/sovereigntist/patriarchal, even if the elements may vary on either side? Such transitions have occurred throughout history: among others, the expansion of Christianity and Islam, the Renaissance, the Enlightenment, the period of colonial conquest and the industrial revolution all brought radical cultural departures in tow. A civilisational crisis has always resulted in a new culture, or, to put it in anthropological terms, deculturation has always been accompanied by acculturation. Often there has been a high price to pay, particularly for dominated groups. These transitions have been experienced differently by the "ancients" and the "moderns." Among conservatives, nostalgia is peppered with lamentations of decadence and a premonition of apocalypse; the end of *a* world has always been perceived as the end of *the* world.[1] Conversely, "progressives" hope for a new world, and glamourise a new culture. Both can be tempted by "authoritarian pedagogy," either to enable them to hold on to the outdated past or to establish a new culture that is not easily imposed.

I argue here for another perspective. We are not in the midst of a cultural transition but a crisis over the very notion of culture. One symptom is the crisis of utopias; another, the extension of normative systems. It is these ideas that I propose to explore.

I shall start by pointing out that today's protest movements are defensive: everyone feels as though they belong to a threatened minority whose rights and spaces must be protected (safe spaces, protest camps, gated communities, national borders). The great universalist utopias are either dead or surviving in desperate radical forms (i.e. all kinds of terrorism). Even the so-called religious revival has failed to reconquer societies and now applies only to individual salvation. Millenarianism has turned into the apocalypse. Far from being a utopia, the fight against climate change is simply an attempt to forestall the coming apocalypse, which others also anticipate under different names. And the only thing that is gradually filling this void with a modicum of hope is a system of regulations, proscriptions and bureaucratic procedures, which the "internet miracle" has merely shifted by turning us into our own bureaucrats, petty fault-finders of ourselves and others, if we want to keep existing at all.

Why are transformations supposedly made in the name of greater individual freedom accompanied by an expanding codification of social practices that considerably shrink "inner" spaces (intimacy, privacy, the unconscious)? I argue that the transformation of "cultures" into explicitly coded systems destroys the notion of culture itself. What I call "coding" is any system designed to make all forms of human communication and relationship unequivocal and linear. The reference to values in this case does not refer to a culture or to an ideal of life, but to the calibration of behaviours according to a vague and muddled reference to normative objectives—such as the "excellence" ranking of universities, to which I will return. Implicit in the extension of normativity are the promotion of "good scores" and the correlative quest for conformism, now systematic in the everyday life of Chinese citizens.

The aim of this book is not to find either a structural or temporal relationship of causality between the four levels. Clearly, there are instances of succession and concomitance. The internet appeared in the wake of 1960s culture and developed alongside financial liberalism, but it was initially commissioned by the army, which was not exactly a haven of Sixties culture. From the 1960s onwards, even as European integration was becoming a reality, the continent encountered waves of immigrant workers. They arrived in a context of de-Christianisation in which they were perceived to actively participate, when in fact it was well underway before they arrived and settled. In another example of ambiguous correlation, financial neoliberalism went hand in hand with the universalist, individualistic Sixties culture, and yet the first political leaders to have imposed it, Reagan and Thatcher, propounded traditional family and religious values. Similarly, contemporary populism may represent libertarian and antireligious values (Geert Wilders in Holland) or by contrast champion the family and religious tradition (the pro-Trump movement in the United States). It would be vain to seek an independent variable and dependent variables (an unfortunately dominant method in social sciences today). We have an array of trends, lifestyles, values, technical innovations and economic practices forming a system that is fluid but often conflictual and chaotic. Trying to detect a plan, a project, or a group in charge of conceiving, predicting and planning our world's transformation would amount to what is termed a conspiracy theory, and which, far from being irrational, cultivates a hyper-rationality with the sole aim of finding the one factor that explains everything.[2]

* * *

I will thus stick to Max Weber's concept of elective affinities (rather than causality) between the Protestant ethic and the spirit of capitalism: Weber never said that capitalism, which already existed in banking form, came about because of Protestantism, or that Protestants were better capitalists than the Catholics or the Jews. He simply noted a deep affinity between the two practices, even if their origins were totally unrelated. Yet this affinity in turn contributed to the development of a coherent system, even the construction of a grand narrative.

Consequently, rather than pondering the causes of elective affinities, I will consider their consequences, and in particular the way in which they can "coagulate," reinforcing one another to produce an effect of legitimation and self-confirmation that makes it more difficult to dispute the tie that binds them. I will look beyond intellectual debates to understand their coherence in everyday life.

THE CRISIS IN QUESTION

Let us now look at the four sequences of civilisational rupture that took place during the single—very short—period between 1960 and 2000; in other words, over the span of a generation (which just happens to be my own).

The May 1968 revolution and the war of values

The 1960s represent a key turning point in the conception of values. It began with a worldwide youth uprising that took various forms (there was nothing hedonistic about the Chinese cultural revolution), but which started in every case by delegitimating the past. The establishment of youth as a specific political category was historically new: in prior revolutionary movements (fascism and communism), while young people formed an avant-garde, they did not constitute an independent category that produced its own values by making a clean break from preceding generations. In the Third World (Asia and Latin America), the 1960s revolts were more political than cultural. In the West, on the other hand, beneath the unsuccessful call for revolution that fizzled out in terrorism (Action Directe, Red Brigades, Baader-Meinhof Group), what finally triumphed was a radical protest against the dominant culture and the values it embodied. At the heart of the struggle was sexuality; it should be remembered that in France, the May 1968 revolts began with male students demanding to be able to enter female dormitories. In the United States, the hippie movement dominated the landscape, including in the protests against the Vietnam War (*Make Love Not War, Peace and Love*, etc.). Cultural demands inspired political involvement rather than the other way round.

How can the originality of the new culture of the 1960s best be described? It was focused on the desiring individual. It was first deeply individualistic, aiming for self-fulfilment by shedding the burden of pre-established constraints and expectations. In a way, it built on Enlightenment ideology, which viewed individuals and their rights as the basis of the social bond formed by the social contract between free subjects who were autonomous with respect to any sort of transcendence. This ties in with Kant, who posited the construction of a new value system based on autonomous reason. But in making the possibility of knowledge the force that offers individuals a way out of their status as "minors" (*sapere aude*, dare to know!), Kant was not breaking with the past. On the contrary, his position reflected the apotheosis of the Enlightenment, for which he provided an argument at once pragmatic ("act in accordance with the maxim") and metaphysical (the impossibility of experiencing transcendence establishes reason as the basis for values). For the 1960s generation—and this is its main innovation with respect to the Enlightenment—desire replaced reason as the basis of autonomy and freedom, leading to a drive for emancipation of an entirely different kind. Pleasure is legitimate in itself. This is, as I showed in *Is Europe Christian?*, a radical departure from Christian culture, even in its secularised version. One could of course claim, as did Foucault, that Christianity did much to construct "sexuality" as a concept broader than a mere physiological need. But what is key here is the axiological reversal—to which psychoanalysis greatly contributed—that transforms sexuality from sin to the path to self-acceptance and self-assertion. We need only remember the slogans of the time: "*jouir sans entraves*," (unfettered pleasure) "*prends tes désirs pour des réalités*" (regard your desires as realities), etc. Individualism is transposed onto the body ("my body is my business"), which has become a value in itself. It is a narcissistic culture indeed.[3]

I use the word revolution because, far from being confined to hippies and protesters, the culture of the desiring individual has become dominant. It was quickly enshrined in the laws and mores of Western societies, whatever the political orientation of those in power in the medium term. In France, birth control pills were authorised under De Gaulle in 1967, abortion under Giscard in 1974. In fact, it was under Giscard's presidency that the definition of family and gender relations were most substantially transformed by law, disconnecting sexuality from procreation and redefining relations between husband and wife as a contractual and egalitarian arrangement. In the United States, a proposed constitutional amendment guaranteeing equality between men and women was passed by a bipartisan majority in Congress in 1972 (but not ratified by the requisite number of states), as was homosexual marriage later in most European countries. A ratchet effect was set in motion: laws expanding sexual freedom, methods of procreation, abortion rights, and changes in marital configurations are almost never abolished by a conservative majority, even if they condemned them while in opposition. Polls show that as regards family mores the libertarian spirit of 1968 transcends party divides and has been on the rise for fifty years.[4]

This is why it makes sense to talk about a change of cultural paradigm, and even of anthropological paradigm, because this change is not based on a political ideology or the rise to power of an authoritarian party. Transformations in the law are in step with those of mores. They are brought about by society, not by a change in government. It is civil society that has changed.

Pope Paul VI instantly grasped the central nature of sexuality in the cultural revolution. He issued the encyclical *Humanae Vitae* in the summer of 1968 to remind the faithful that sexuality was reserved for marital fidelity and procreation. American evangelicals took a bit more time to react, placing the abortion issue at the heart of their combat against the new mores, whereas it had not featured in their preaching prior to the 1970s.[5] The 1970s saw the development of what became known in the West as "culture wars", which take various forms depending on the country. I see the phenomenon more as a "war of values,"

15

because it is waged within Western culture itself. It is the opposite of a "clash of civilisations," which supposedly pits a relatively unified "Western culture" against other cultures. These so-called culture wars were analysed by James D. Hunter in a fundamental study of the same name.[6]

In the United States the division is very clear. It took shape with the 1964 election campaign in relation to the Republican presidential candidate Barry Goldwater: on one side, a Republican conservative strand, very reticent toward the civil rights movement that had inflamed the country under Martin Luther King's leadership; on the other, the Democrats, open to the new values of emancipation and minority rights. In the wake of Goldwater's failed bid for the presidency, the Christian right led by the evangelicals picked up the torch and ensured Ronald Reagan's win in 1980; a similar mix put Trump in the White House in 2016.

These societal issues are not correlated to economic or geostrategic choices. For instance, the US Republican Party has been by turns interventionist and isolationist, in favour of free trade or the return of tariffs. Conservative values focus on the traditional family, the complementarity of sex roles, opposition to abortion and subsequently to same-sex marriage. Not all religious people belong to the Christian coalition, far from it, but liberal believers refuse to make their faith a public issue, unlike right-wing evangelicals.

In Europe, the Catholic Church spearheads opposition to the new values. While Pope Paul VI's *Humanae Vitae* was theoretically directed only at Catholics, forty years later Pope Benedict XVI championed "non-negotiable moral principles"—life in all its stages, family, religious freedom—at each of his meetings with European parliamentarians and other political figures. Catholic philosophers such as Pierre Manent and Marcello Pera advocate a return to the concept of natural law to counter what they consider the excesses of human rights theory that is allegedly not based on any transcendent value. Within a largely dechristianised society, the Catholic Church is trying to find arguments that convince others besides the faithful. In their view, the non-negotiable moral principles are not merely the expression of divine law since, according to the great theologian Thomas Aquinas, they reflect natural law, and abandoning them would amount to destroying the anthropological principles of human society.[7]

The problem for the Catholic Church in Europe is that, since the end of the halcyon days of Christian democracy, it has lacked a political intermediary (except in Poland): the major parties representing the classic right (the English Conservative Party, the German CDU, the French RPR and later the Spanish PPP and the Irish Fianna Fáil) surrendered to the new state of public opinion, whereas Christian Democrats lost their place on the political chessboard because their loyalty to the Catholic Church's social doctrine prevented them from championing the prevailing neoliberalism. The neoliberal right ratified the new Sixties values, much to the dismay of conservatives, who were increasingly relegated to the minority.[8] In the West at least, the turning tide of public opinion was striking: in Ireland, the criminalisation of abortion was enshrined in the Constitution in 1983 with 63% of the vote, but a generation later, in 2018, the freedom to have an abortion was passed with an identical majority. In California, same-sex marriage was rejected by referendum in 2008 but reinstated by the courts in 2013, whereas the US Supreme Court authorised it in 2015, even though the majority of judges were Republicans. The only backsliding on issues such as abortion and LGBT rights has been due to the activism of a Supreme Court run by the conservative right. It does not reflect a change in public opinion, which remains liberal regarding the issue of mores. In western Europe, neither Marine Le Pen, nor Matteo Salvini, nor Geert Wilders, nor even Éric Zemmour want to go back on the issues of abortion and same-sex marriage.[9] On the other hand, in the United States, the Christian right has seized control of the Republican Party, through Trump, without having made significant headway in public opinion.

The conservative right recognised its defeat, deploring the change in mores that had driven the West into decline. The iconic book in this regard (even if the author refuses to be pigeonholed on the right) is Allan Bloom's *The Closing of the American Mind*, published in the United States in 1987; Rod Dreher's more recent *The Benedict Option: A Strategy for Christians in a Post-Christian Nation* (2017), which was quickly translated into several European languages, confirms that Christians are henceforth in the minority and can no longer impose their values. As Ross Douthat, a conservative editorialist with the *New York Times*, admits, "The 'Jesusland' that showed up in liberal memes after the 2004 election has been shrinking ever since, and socially liberal values have advanced on a wide range of issues."[10]

The disconnect between political orientation and moral options is particularly visible in attitudes toward the economy. It became apparent in the 1970s that values associated with globalisation and neoliberalism (individualism, hedonism, "everything is possible," "do it yourself," self-improvement, cosmopolitism) are closer to those of the Sixties revolutionaries than to those of conservatives.

Lastly, it is worth noting now, because I will return to it, that the backlash that began around 2010 against the excessive permissiveness of 1968 (tolerance for paedophilia, sexual freedom used for male domination) has not involved a return to traditional values, but has occurred within the Sixties paradigm itself and in the name of its ideals of individualism and freedom. What has come under fire, particularly by feminists, is the perpetuation of power relations under cover of promoting desire, understood as the exuberant (male) libido. Far from promoting the traditional family, the #MeToo campaign is part of an even more radical critique of the heterosexual couple. #MeToo is not a new puritanism, but an attempt to diminish the contradiction inherent in the principle of freedom.

The Sixties model seems essentially "white" and is embodied by the babyboomer generation, who experienced unprecedented economic expansion. It is therefore thought to be a basically Western phenomenon. And yet, the Sixties "culture" soon went global. The new aspect here was that this worldwide spread was not driven by the dominant culture but primarily by "subcultures": music, youth culture, alternative media (and later Facebook, Twitter, Instagram, TikTok, etc.), in other words tools that could instantly be used by the "dominated". Similarly, the English language has spread through the democratisation of its use worldwide (the exact opposite of the globalisation of French in the eighteenth century, which was a result of aristocratic mores—French nannies were a must!) and the same phenomenon has occurred with food (fast food, from McDonald's to kebab shops), furniture (IKEA) and streetwear. At this juncture, it is worth pointing out that the post-Sixties globalisation is not a form of acculturation to a "major" culture, but the dissemination of a series of codes. This coding of everyday life has become independent from the original cultures in which it has arrived, and self-replicates in the virtual space.

The conservative reaction to the spirit of May 1968 is "reactive", not to say reactionary. It yearns to return to a prior state and is played out in the mode of mournful, authoritarian nostalgia. Depending on whether it leans left or right, it aims to return either to the republican pact (the social contract within the nation-state framework), or the grounding of culture in transcendence, which may be religious or understood as an exalted, intangible human nature. The left's problem is to define the group to which the social contract applies. This explains its nostalgia for the nation state and its borders, because the social contract, on which life in society is founded, no longer functions in social systems in which domination is diffuse. The social contract then looks more like a myth that masks processes of alienation and domination.[11] As for conservatives, who have never accepted the theory of the social contract, they either repeat the same old song about the people, race or ethnic group or they refer to the divine order. They are thwarted by the accelerated secularisation of the modern world and the dissolution of the religious quest in favour of the search for individual happiness.[12] Both camps want to rehabilitate culture (high culture being its most accomplished form), but they clash with the de facto alliance between the post-1968 spirit and neoliberalism.

Failure is therefore inherent in the goal of both conservatives and partisans of the Enlightenment and the nation-state. Any victory that is not founded on a shared imaginary can only be imposed by an authority or the hypothetical conversion of a majority of the population, which would be nothing short of miraculous.[13] Authoritarian "re-education" never works, especially in an internet-based world, while miracles only occur in moments of catastrophe—for which some might even hope. Narratives of decline often share a fascination for the apocalypse, possibly in the form of a coming civil war.[14]

In fact, the normative system unfolding today is grounded more in neoliberalism than in civic or religious nostalgia.

Neoliberalism: commodification and offshoring

Neoliberalism is the across-the-board implementation of a free market that no longer relies on production but rather on the financialisation and systematic commodification of everything that is not necessarily merchandise. Our focus here will not be on its specifically economic aspects, or even its political implications, but rather on the impact of neoliberalist expansion in the field of culture and values.[15]

Marx had already envisaged the commodification of the world by capitalism, but within certain limits: a use value and a labour value were still required for an object or service to qualify as a "commodity." The market economy today pays no heed to these limits: an exchange value is all that remains.

The extension of the domain of commodification to the private sphere is illustrated by reality television shows (*Loft Story* was a pioneer of the genre in France and serves as a paradigm for all subsequent forms of self-exposure, particularly in social media): every aspect, or nearly, of a person's everyday life should be visible without mediation or selection. Everywhere, emotions are codified, classified and weighted: the old Latin concept of *pretium doloris* ("the price of pain") now applies to the slightest annoyance, for which one can be indemnified—as long as one can prove one's suffering, show it and measure it, place it on a scale. NFTs (non-fungible tokens) imply that any "object," taken out of its context or its use, can be assigned a market value without it even being converted into a work of art (for instance, as Marcel Duchamp did by exhibiting a urinal in a museum). It is a token: an object of exchange devoid of content, with no claim to having meaning (as opposed to modern artworks, even the most "vacuous" or "vain," such as those by Jeff Koons, with his kitsch *Bouquet of Tulips* meant as a tribute to the victims of the November 2015 attacks in Paris). Exchange value has replaced use value.

The register of emotions is thus reduced to a collection of tokens. Eva Illouz provides a remarkable demonstration of how emotions have been commodified, both in the development of various psychotherapies and in the evaluation of mental suffering, with an aim to establish claims for damages.[16] The need to measure and protect these new commodities is thus an extension of normativity and adjudication. This normativity has no axiological purpose (no "good"): it is a norm with no "value" (but with a price to pay); such is the paradox of neoliberalism.[17]

The most visible impact of neoliberalism is the crisis in the social bond, alongside the deterritorialisation it implies. Keynesian economic theory, which dominated the Western world after the Second World War, proposed a new social contract between capital and labour, based on permanent negotiation between unions and employers. It therefore encouraged recognition of a working class rooted in a territory, wholly involved in the national political process (social democracy or Christian democracy) and valued for its productive activity. It was based on the assumption that the economy was grounded in a social reality (a social status), a political reality (representation through political parties), and even an anthropological reality (the development of working-class subcultures).

The financialisation of the economy to the detriment of production tears up these roots. Deterritorialisation occurs through the offshoring of business activities and corporations, thus removing the site of social class and social conflict, but also that of the social compact. Offshoring does not mean that an industry is relocated elsewhere and recreates the social bond: it remains nomadic and produces nothing but unstable jobs. But there is a link between territorialisation, socialisation and shared culture (whether it is a culture in the anthropological sense or simply a subculture). Working-class cultures no longer have the social and territorial base needed to develop: in France, for instance, we have seen the disappearance of employee councils organising recreation for workers, particularly company holiday camps for children, which promoted socialisation. The replacement of the employee by the individual as entrepreneur blurs class boundaries and gives the illusion that everyone can be an entrepreneur, while making those individuals responsible for managing their own lack of job security (Uberisation). This is what Bernard Harcourt pointed out: "Facebook assumes and promotes the idea of the entrepreneurial self, so closely tied to Chicago School theories of human capital," in other words, neoliberalism.[18]

Space is not the only thing at issue in deterritorialisation: time is as well. As Aristotle said, though in a different way, culture requires a degree of leisure, in other words a period of detachment from work (which prevents too much instability and mobility) and some form of collective life.[19] This time has vanished: there is no longer a barrier between work and private life, because work is no longer a collective endeavour. Remote working and the lockdowns imposed by Covid19 merely systematised a long-range trend and made it commonplace. In this regard, the pandemic is deeply modern.

Neoliberalism weakens the nation-state because the state no longer has the means (and often no longer the will) to intervene in the economic sphere, over whose actors and rationale it has no grasp; it has no control over the forces of globalisation. A local element (tribe, sect, peer network, advocacy group, piece of territory) can connect to the global level without going through the intermediary of the state: this is *glocalisation*. Neoliberalism is not interested in the social bond. Margaret Thatcher put this anthropological viewpoint in a nutshell when she declared, as quoted by David Harvey, that there was "no such thing as society, only individual men and women and their families." Harvey says of neoliberal thought that "all forms of social solidarity were to be dissolved in favour of individualism, private property, personal responsibility and family values."[20] In this, Thatcher represents the essential paradox of the neoliberal conservative politician: in politics, she claimed to champion traditional values (including the family); she was anti-abortion and anti-LGBTQ; she praised the value of work as opposed to welfare dependency; and yet her anthropological stance destroyed the social base of her values, and notably the social base of British working class culture, which would never recover from the failure of the great miners' strike of 1984. In fact, very quickly (as of the 1980s), the social-democrats espoused neoliberalism which they linked to the libertarian values of 1968 (this was the case for instance of advisors to Mitterrand, Schröder, and Blair), whereas a new liberal right, as already pointed out, ditched respect for traditional values (Berlusconi replaced Christian democracy by the new right, good manners by blingbling and bungabunga,[21] and art by kitsch, as Trump would do subsequently). That the conservative Christian right backs candidates whose personal lives in no way conform to its values (Marine Le Pen, Zemmour, Salvini, Berlusconi, Trump) is paradoxical only in appearance: their discourse is conservative, but in their personal behaviour they embody the new values they challenge. The GAFAM companies (now GAMAM, since Facebook became Meta) and the internet are a perfect example of this merger of neoliberalism and libertarian values. Later, these big tech companies would enthusiastically endorse these new values and try to outdo one another in their inclusiveness. As Daniel Cohen writes, "the restoration promised by the conservative revolution may have been understood as a return to the founding values of capitalism, those of the Puritans, but it ushered in the opposite: the triumph of greed."[22] This congruence between neoliberalism and Sixties values has not eluded the two types of critiques directed at it: one from the right, the other from the left (Christopher Lasch regarding narcissism, Michéa, McIntyre, Botz-Bornstein on kitsch, Carole Pateman on the sexual contract, Eva Illouz on the commodification of private life). Labour is no longer a value (as it was in both senses of the term under capitalism); success is the value (the concept of excellence). Yet as success can only be measured through competition and comparison with others, it is self-referential, and in this regard closely linked to narcissism:

individuals display their value the better to prove it, for it rests on nothing but comparison and thus largely on performance, which might help explain the incredible race for wealth among already very rich corporate executives who can only enjoy their wealth through the eyes of others. Ostentation thus replaces the accumulation of capital. A puritan can no longer be a capitalist.

The blurring of the distinction between left and right is hence complete: in economics, the glorification of the free market is no longer the province of the right, and state interventionism is no longer the preserve of the left. Opposition to globalisation can come from the left or the right (as can the defence of universalism), and regarding the issue of values, populist parties (such as Rassemblement National) do not necessarily represent conservative values (family, sexuality). All that matters to them is to designate an irreconcilable Other (for instance Islam) that ensures an identity for the good people, which the Other itself does not enjoy. The blurring of left and right is the consequence of a crisis of political culture, itself an integral part of the crisis of culture in general.

The internet: a self-referential virtual world

Most of the major works deploring the crisis of values (the previously mentioned prototype being Allan Bloom's *Closing of the American Mind*) or observing the crisis of culture (Guy Debord and Jean Baudrillard) were written before the internet boom. The internet is thus not the cause of cultural breakdown, but provides the means for it to mutate. The internet does not create narcissistic individualism but gives it an unprecedented space within which it can unfurl, with wide-ranging communication, direct contact, networks, do-it-yourself videos, MySpace, the construction and performance of self, Facebook, My Life, affinity groups. The internet substitutes an unmediated virtual, global and accessible space for the old territorialised and socialised world. Social life is no longer tied to the place where one lives or even the physical reality surrounding the user; the internet knows nothing of strong social bonds, for it offers a disembodied bond that never approaches individuals holistically but considers only that part of them that they choose to engage. If to choose means to make explicit, then people do not choose to show their dark side; that is the aspect they try to ignore. People choose only what they want to be, with no social determinism. There is no feedback from reality, at least when one is online. Of course, there is still the rent to pay, the workday to get through, the kids to pick up from school and so on, but social constraints are seen as optional or marginal. Reality does not vanish but becomes secondary. Individuals are no longer grounded in a social fabric. That does not mean they have no friends, family or relations, but that they dissociate work, sociability and the cultural (or subcultural) sphere.

How does the internet cause a crisis in the very idea of culture? That is the question I am interested in here. To my mind, it does not so much create an "internet culture" as a system of representations and relations that oppose the very notion of culture, as the internet is based on the systematic coding of communication and the constant explication of content. Only literal meanings matter. Anything meant humorously or tongue-in-cheek must be signaled by an emoticon that indicates one is joking or that one is outraged. But explicating irony amounts to reverting to the literal meaning.

To my mind, the main feature of the internet is its self-referential dimension. An algorithm does not make anything up: it anticipates based on what is known, it rummages horizontally through all the available data to define profiles. The term "profile" is interesting in itself, because a profile is by definition a drawing without depth that aims to represent only what is explicit in a person, using a finite number of preselected traits. While a portrait should leave an element of mystery and exceptionality about a person, a profile requires no interpretation or doubt. It should instantly convey an unequivocal meaning through a finite amount of information. Profiles are never far from stereotypes, even caricature.[23]

The problem is not so much that the internet encourages everyone to frequent only likeminded people (this is just as much a tendency in real life), but that peer affinities are constructed by algorithms. We don't know if these affinities would function in real life, because reality is always mediated by something else: other people, families, work, territory, and so on. The internet is unaffected by such mediation. Incidentally, this manner of reducing a person to a certain number of stable, autonomous traits is also found in today's quantitative sociology, which strives to isolate individuals by their specific opinions (most of the time with a view to predicting how they will vote), in order to group them into categories that have less and less to do with their sociological background, but rather in terms of opinions (the list of which is previously defined by the investigator). The internet is certainly an aspect of this widespread change of cultural perspective in society.

Languages are known to be the repositories of cultures. For a long time, the internet came up against the obstacle of languages, which is only logical, but the obstacle has been circumvented. The internet does not aim to achieve the best possible Turkish translation of *In Search of Lost Time*, but to convert the novel into something that can be read in all contexts, in short, to extract it from the category of "literature". This is how the internet decontextualises languages and thus simplifies them.

The internet world therefore refers only back to itself, and it is this self-referentiality that makes it impossible for an internet culture, in both senses of the word (anthropological and literary), to take hold, to the benefit of a subculture in a world deprived of high culture. This aspect will be broached in the following chapter.

With its virtual worlds, individualisation and construction of the individual on the model of "profile" and "peers" (via the agglutination of explicit markers), its bypassing of national cultures by transforming real languages (which can be used online once they have been "sterilised") into a metalanguage that makes them interchangeable, its desocialisation, auto-referentiality and systematic coding, the internet is not inventing a new culture; it is destroying the very idea of culture. Its ultimate logic is probably to make any reference to reality useless by creating metaverses, in other words virtual and self-sufficient worlds.

Crisis of the nation-state and all-out mobility: the de-Westernisation of the world

Globalisation, in its many different forms, is a fact that one can deplore, take note of or use to good advantage. I will not go into a description of the phenomenon but simply recall a few well-known aspects: crisis of the nation-state, open borders (de jure or de facto), the globalisation of the market and consumer tastes, the role of multinationals and investment funds, migrations, the status of English as a global language, the deterritorialisation of the academic world and the job market, and the shrinking of space and time, particularly owing to the drop in the cost of plane tickets, and the accessibility of nearly all four corners of the world, if not physically then at least via Google Earth and other tools for visualising and zooming in on locations.

Globalisation is usually perceived as a problem of interculturality. Huntington's famous "clash of civilisations" of course comes to mind, but its apparent opposite, a dialogue of civilisations, is based on the same premise. The world is divided up into various

THE CRISIS IN QUESTION

supposedly homogeneous spaces, defined at the highest level as "civilisations," whose distinguishing criterion is based on cultures that have emerged from the secularisation of religions—one can be Christian without believing in God, but still refer to a Christian identity.

This culturalist vision often appears in migrant integration policies: the debate between multiculturalism and assimilationism basically assumes a similar vision of cultural ensembles that were once distinct and distant but are now juxtaposed by the movement of populations. Should we accept the juxtaposition of cultures in new spaces, or should we promote integration into the dominant culture? In both cases, it often boils down to asking if these cultures are "compatible." Such culturalist views, which are based on the idea that cultures exist and that they largely determine people's practices, emphasise the importance, criticised or desired, of cultural "territories" in the host country (from Chinatown to the "lost territories of the republic"—areas / segments of the public sphere allegedly abandoned by the state).

The problem is that the theme of cultural compatibility arises precisely at a time when all cultures are undergoing a deculturation process, with widely differing effects. There is symmetry in deculturation but not in the reconfiguration process, in other words in the establishment of new systems of values and normativity. Deculturation is reflected in a recourse to weak identities constructed through a handful of markers (red wine and sausage, headscarf and halal) detached from their context, and in a crisis of high cultures.

Is globalisation thus the expression of a worldwide Westernisation or instead the triumph of barbarians? And if the latter, who are the new barbarians? The key question is whether globalisation is occurring to the advantage of Western culture (the viewpoint of postcolonial studies) or bringing about an "Americanisation" of the world (the viewpoint of European identitarians,

29

who are as much against immigration from the southern hemisphere as they are opposed to the cultural influence of the United States, or what is seen as such in "woke" cultures: neo-feminists, intersectionalists and deconstructionists), or whether we are witnessing a *sui generis* process of widespread deculturation (my argument). Interestingly, whereas postcolonial studies theory in the tradition of Edward Saïd assumes a relative unity of the West, European populists and nationalists see American culture and multiculturalism as two accomplices that together are undermining traditional European culture.

What, then, is the West? Is it one culture among many others, which has insured its supremacy since its expansion overseas in 1492, or is it the cradle of a value system that emerged in the Enlightenment and claims to be universal in scope, in other words above all culture, starting with its very own? Since the United Nations issued the Universal Declaration of Human Rights in 1948, the main Sixties values—sexual freedom, secularisation (and thus the right to blasphemy), the championing of feminism and later gay rights—have in turn been redefined as "human rights" and ratified in Western law and in the political discourse. They have thus become the hallmark of the West that conservative cultures and religions oppose: McDonald's versus jihad soon came to represent the clash of civilisations in all its various manifestations after Huntington.

It is a case of one thing or the other: either the promotion of so-called Western values (human rights, democracy, rule of law, secularisation, even feminism) is merely another way of ensuring the West's cultural hegemony, or these values have become autonomous with respect to the culture that spawned them and they now form a universalist system of thought picked up by movements calling for democracy from Tiananmen Square to Tahrir Square, from Beijing to Cairo. The first critique is central to cultural studies and postcolonial studies, which for instance deny that the purpose of the ban on the Muslim headscarf (*hijab*) in French schools is women's liberation, instead maintaining that it actually discriminates against the Muslim community. Far from liberating people, secularisation, and particularly the rigorous separation of religion from the state, known in France as *laïcité*, are said to be instruments of cultural domination over societies that have a different view of the place of religion in culture and politics. The opposing viewpoint upholds the universality of the values of law and freedom (sexual, among others) and points to the robustness of democratic movements in other, non-Western cultures as evidence. But two opposing movements in the West itself dispute this Western claim to embody the new liberal values: on one hand, populists and Christian traditionalists alike challenge liberalism and the West's universalist conceit (because the corollary of universalism is faith in the integration of migrants from other cultures); on the other, in this same Western culture, feminists excoriate the persistence of a patriarchal culture that de facto excludes women from the social contract. And to complicate things further, champions of multiculturalism suspect this same feminism of being too white and condescending toward Muslim women, while transgender advocates have recently attacked feminism for its reluctance to consider trans people as women. In short, the conflict over values is not a conflict between cultures, but an attempt to conceptualise values above and beyond culture. As these values do not correspond to a shared implicit understanding, they have to be imposed. And these conflicts of course play a role in structuring political divides.

In this "crisis of culture", diagnosed by many, I would therefore like to examine the very notion of culture. The term calls up various meanings, but all of them revolve around two poles: culture in the anthropological sense, in other words the common framework of meaning and representations specific to a

31

given society or community, and culture as canon (or high culture), a set of intellectual or artistic productions selected and considered "good" to know or to practise. The former is implicit (and must be "decoded" by society itself or by the anthropologist studying it); the latter is explicit and thus implies the task of selection and transmission.

My argument is that, rather than a mere crisis of culture, what we are now witnessing is the "deculturation of cultures": a dissolution of the content of the cultural canon, an obliteration of anthropological cultures, and the paradoxical promotion (through globalisation) of "subcultures" that are autonomous from the dominant culture within which they were embedded but are now reduced to codes of communication disconnected from real cultures. This is what I will scrutinise in the following chapters.

2

ANTHROPOLOGICAL CULTURE

THE ERASURE OF SHARED IMPLICIT
UNDERSTANDINGS

All societies rely on a shared system of language, signs, symbols, representations of the world, body language, behavioural codes, and so on. This common framework in no way implies a consensus on values or political choices: conflicts and tensions can be exacerbated to the point of breaking a society apart, representations change, new worldviews appear and revolutions bring about radical change, not to mention the full range of individual variations within the same society. But from the start there is always an implicit system of representations and symbols that make communication possible. Language precedes grammar: people speak before knowing how to speak correctly. This is what I mean by the implicit dimension of culture, and there can be no culture without it. Lang.- rlc.

Culture in the anthropological sense creates *habitus*, implicit rules of the game, a sort of self-evidence, a "normal" state. From this implicitness, every culture attempts to clarify itself through language, to account for itself. It specifies "good manners," it

3

"imagines" models of men and women to emulate, it elaborates a pedagogy and techniques of transmission: proverbs, songs, stories, myths, literature, arts, philosophy and law. It projects itself in an imaginary. When this happens, values and norms are no longer implicit but are put into words. There is thus a dialectical relationship between *habitus* and values: in societies where honour is important, anger rises quickly; in those that favour self-control, revenge is exacted at a later time. But the act of explication always aims to bring out what is implicit; it does not claim to mark a departure from it. There is hence a coherence between implicit and explicit: like a cookbook, grammar (explicit codes) claims to state what is "true" about its own culture by putting that truth through the mill of norms; it is not autonomous with respect to the anthropological culture, but offers a distilled, refined, purified version of it. There is thus a dialectic relationship between implicit and explicit, between norms and values, between the social bond and the imaginary.[1]

This cultural imaginary is in crisis. It is taking the form of a deculturation that is not followed by an acculturation, in other words access to a new culture.

Deculturation without acculturation

Deculturation is a frequent phenomenon throughout history, but it is always followed by acculturation: Gallic society and its language have disappeared, but Gallic populations blended into a new Roman (and hardly Gallic) ensemble. The process today is more complex. It is not only the dominated who are losing their culture, but the dominant cultures are also in crisis. I also see the challenges to dominant cultures posed by deconstructionism, cultural studies and postcolonial studies more as symptoms of the crisis than as agents of the decline of those cultures.

In this broad anthropological process, deculturation is of course more visible in dominated groups: immigrants, indigenous societies, the working class. Immigrants do not remain long in diaspora: a crisis begins for "immigrant cultures" as early as the second generation and they in turn undergo their own deconstruction, even if the populists' favourite argument (and this is unfortunately true of some sociologists) is that the culture of origin persists in subsequent immigrant generations. Deculturation is a slow and often painful process when the opportunities for accessing the dominant culture are blocked. Anthropologists are familiar with the "lumpenisation" of primitive societies: the Inuit in the Canadian Great North, the Indian reservations in the United States, and the Aborigines in Australia are afflicted by alcoholism, unemployment and drug abuse. Jonathan Lear's book *Radical Hope* very perceptively describes how an Indian tribe, the Crows, which in the late nineteenth century chose to side with the United States Army against other tribes (and therefore were not victims of massacres or spoliation), suddenly found themselves in a totally different social and economic world: one that made their culture obsolete, useless and empty. Talking about the moment when the tribe had to give up hunting and making war, their chief told the researcher: "after this nothing happened." The Indians may have learned to employ the codes of their new society (the chief, Plenty Coups, had become a regular visitor to Washington, where he wore his feather headdress and represented the "good Indian" who upheld the United States Constitution), but everyday life had lost its meaning. It was mere survival. There was no imaginary left in life.[2]

Likewise, the crisis of class-specific cultures (small farmers, the working class) has not escaped sociologists or novelists. Richard Hoggart, an English sociologist himself from a working-class background, discusses this with regard to "class defectors":

> They are much affected by the cynicism which affects nearly everyone, but this is likely to increase their lack of purpose rather than tempt them to 'cash in' or to react into further indulgence. [...] With

them the sense of loss is increased precisely because they are emo-
tionally uprooted from their class, often under the stimulus of a
stronger critical intelligence or imagination, qualities which can lead
them into an unusual self-consciousness before their own situation
(and make it easy for a sympathizer to dramatize their Angst).
Involved with this may be a physical uprooting from their class
through the medium of the scholarship system. A great many seem
to me to be affected in this way, though only a very small proportion
badly; at one boundary the group includes psychotics; at the other,
people leading apparently normal lives but never without an underlying sense of some unease.[3]

Class defectors have to face a dominant class sure of its values.
But what happens when the dominant class no longer embod-
ies values and whole categories of the population lose their cultural bearings, even when they are not necessarily "dominated"?
That is where we are today. The sociologist Laurent Bouvet
diagnosed this malaise, labelling it "cultural insecurity", a term
onto which the populists have latched, naturally attributing it to
external destabilising forces: immigrants, and in particular
Muslims.[4] Yet this phenomenon has deeper roots and is found in
several parts of the world. How is it, for instance, that in a society such as India, where Hindus are easily the majority of the
population and are politically and culturally dominant (the
Muslim minority is the poorest), cultural insecurity could
develop to the extent of putting the Bharatiya Janata Party (BJP,
the big Hindu nationalist party) in power in 2014, with Narendra
Modi as prime minister? How can "White Americans," who hold
an overwhelming majority of economic and political power in the
United States (we need only look at a photograph of the US
Congress), feel threatened by real minorities, who live in far
greater insecurity, not only in cultural terms but also in relation
to their physical circumstances and even their lives? If everyone
feels culturally insecure, then the crisis is much deeper: then
there is no new common culture to be seen on the horizon.

Anthropologists had identified this insecurity only among dominated groups, which went from deculturation to acculturation under the aegis of the dominant group. Now, dominant groups are overwhelmed by cultural anxiety: if they feel threatened by the dominated, it is firstly because they have considerable trouble defining their own culture. For instance, what "European values" can we offer immigrants or assert to counter theirs when the Commission of the Bishops' Conferences of the European Union and the European Parliament are unable to agree on such basic things as the definition of the family, sexual freedom and gender? How can Europe's Christian identity be asserted when popes keep denouncing Europe's paganism? I will return to the issue of "values" and "cultures" being reduced to folklorised identity traits in Chapter 4.

Sociability devoid of content

The crisis of culture is of course linked to the crisis in the social bond and the disconnect between shared imaginaries and social life. Desocialisation, individualisation and deterritorialisation are the three key elements. The sociological foundation required for a culture to exist is in crisis. It has not disappeared; there are still nations, societies, social classes, socio-occupational groups, ethnic groups, tribes, villages, neighbourhoods and so on. But these sociological affiliations are increasingly dissociated from forms of virtual sociability that have developed through the use of the internet.

The harshest occurrences in real life (a pandemic or a war such as the Russian aggression against Ukraine, for example) are no longer enough to bring people back to reality. Thus, the conspiracy bubble functions (and attracts a large swathe of the population, even if it is difficult to quantify) by virtually sharing an imaginary that is self-confirmed by people who recognise each other beyond cultures and in total indifference to the environment in which they live. This type of "subculture" has become autonomous.

Desocialisation occurs when individuals are no longer involved in a web of real social relations that structure their various activities: work, leisure, sexuality, meals and so on. These activities no longer necessarily need to be performed within a social framework. Desocialisation can even be pathological, as it is with the Japanese *hikikomori*, young adults who live with their parents and no longer leave their rooms, living only in front of their screens. One might argue of course that this phenomenon remains marginal from a sociological standpoint (around 300,000 people in Japan) and can thus be treated as a pathology and not as a feature of society. But its significance is not quantitative: the fascination that the *hikikomori* exercise and the way in which many young people pretend to be like them turns the phenomenon if not into an ideal type, at least into a possible pole of identification, an imaginary projection of themselves onto a heroic figure. We should note that this virtual sociability is based on codes rather than on content—it is striking, for instance, that brevity has become the main standard for all communication, on Twitter, TikTok and in speed dating. It would be wrong to see this as superficial: life is no less intense in the virtual than in the real world (to wit: the brutality of verbal exchanges and their often tragic consequences, such as teenage suicide). Levelling does not necessarily imply superficiality: a flat surface can engage the same amount of vital energy as depth. What is being levelled is the distance, the distinction between the virtual and the real, between speech and action. We are in a world that is more performative than ever, where speech is action. The declarative world is replacing the world of action.

ANTHROPOLOGICAL CULTURE

The disappearance of shared territory

Such desocialisation coincides with deterritorialisation, which is a consequence of the loss of attachment to particular localities (such as villages and neighbourhoods) and to the nation-state, and here again of globalisation and the expansion of the internet. This crisis harbours a paradox: the more shared territory vanishes, the more the defence of territory becomes an obsession, but then the territories are segmented into disconnected entities. Never has there been so much talk about territory since deterritorialisation: from the "lost territories of the Republic" (see above) to protest camps, and including "safe spaces" (where one feels secure among peers), and gated communities, whether they are in Chinatown, downtown Manhattan, or the very Catholic Monasphère.[5] Recent immigrants and minority religious groups have naturally been held responsible for this fragmentation of shared space and the tendency to withdraw into a territory where they only meet others of their own kind (which is nothing new: ghettos and ethnic neighbourhoods have always existed). But what is striking is that the movement has diversified, now—and soon mainly?—affecting the "dominators". The US journalist Rod Dreher even theorised the phenomenon for Christians in his book *The Benedict Option: A Strategy for Christians in a Post-Christian Nation*; now that Christians are a minority, they should group together to live, work, and protect their faith, as the early Benedictine monks did.[6] He threw his support behind the Monasphère project in France.[7] In the United States, white supremacists are also working to create areas reserved for whites.[8] The Supreme Court ruling in June 2022 which overturned the right to abortion allows conservative states to impose their own normative system on their territory, thereby departing from the federal system. But such attempts to take over territory are not the sole province of conservatives: Democrats and extreme leftist activists have also undertaken more temporary occupations, in what the geographer Michel Lussault named "the struggle in the squares."[9] But can the protests that took place in public spaces during the Arab Spring in Egypt and in Tunisia in 2010–11, those of the "colour revolutions"[10] backed by the West in Georgia, Ukraine, and Kyrgyzstan between 2003–06, Occupy Wall Street and other Occupy protests, and the safe spaces on US campuses banning remarks likely to offend a category of occupants all be lumped together? Major critics of neoliberalism, such as David Graeber, have been fervent supporters of the Occupy movement. But occupying a place does not really have much impact. It is more a staged protest than a real social movement because people join in on an individual basis. What is lacking is precisely the sociological grounding, the shared motive that made workers in 1936 or in 1968 occupy their factories. Cultural insecurity, by contrast, results in a sort of self-ghettoisation, even in public demonstrations and including in places that are paradoxically places of passage, such as the squares and the roundabouts occupied by the Gilets Jaunes (Yellow Vests), going around in circles in a barbecue atmosphere. Even during the Arab Spring, the crowds on the squares of Tunis and Cairo did not generate lasting political movements. The demonstrators spurned any potential leader or political framework and instead relished the often festive spirit of the protest. Only the "colour revolutions" in the Middle East and in Central Asia have had lasting political consequences, but they have not made the transition to structured political movements with a programme, or even an ideology. Crucially, they have not given rise to any local form of activism, systematic deployment of activists throughout the territory, involvement in trade unions or existing social organisations, not to mention their failure to create new political organisations.[11] In all cases, the changing relationship to territory requires the culture to be reformatted as a subculture linked to a self-defined group of likeminded people.

ANTHROPOLOGICAL CULTURE

Denigrators of "multiculturalism," who in France are found among both the conservative and populist right and the "republic-minded left," focus almost solely on "Islamist separatism": they denounce the formation of self-sufficient "ecosystems" cut off from the society that encompasses them and to which they are often hostile, holding up their own system of norms and values in opposition. But to my mind, this separatism does not result from a strategy, because the Salafists have no strategic vision and the Muslim Brotherhood has little impact on underprivileged neighbourhoods. It is the product of the collapse of shared space that affects everyone, as shown by some sociologists who cannot be said to sympathise with the Islamists, such as Christophe Guilluy or Jérôme Fourquet. The trial relating to the 13 November 2015 attacks in Paris amply demonstrated this: it began with the assumption that the perpetrators came from a Salafist ecosystem comprising in this case the town of Molenbeek, Belgium, but it gradually became apparent that they had no ties with a hypothetical "Muslim community", instead living in a much smaller and far less religious bubble: the Béguines Café, where drugs and alcohol were consumed and Islamist videos of decapitation were viewed. There are hence no homogeneous territories—Salafist neighbourhoods, peri-urban areas where poor white people supposedly live, poor rural villages—there are only places, intersections, passages and roundabouts. This general deterritorialisation can of course be called an illusion. War instantly brings a territory back to life through the movement of troops, occupation, and the flight of refugees. But contemporary wars are all unfinished: whether they end with a treaty or linger on for years with repeated skirmishes and precarious ceasefires, they still produce more refugees, deny the existence of peoples and leave patchwork territories, enclaves, red lines (always crossed) and grey areas: Bosnia, Kashmir, Syria, Western Sahara, Georgia and Armenia, Ethiopia, and soon probably Ukraine. Cities are divided (Beirut, Sarajevo) and refugee camps become permanent.

States happily outsource local conflicts to militias, mercenaries and private enterprises that do more to sow chaos than to bring order. None of these wars have re-established the territorial order, secured the periphery, or called forth new empires. Many leaders are haunted by ghostly territories, but their dream of rebuilding an empire only creates an even more ragtag world. The modern state that grew out of the Westphalian order brought together a sovereign, a territory, a people and a religion (secularised in a political culture): today, both its institutions and its territorial base are teetering.

These patchwork territories also haunt fiction, where they raise the spectre of civil war and secession within the very heart of the West. The US television miniseries *DMZ*, for instance, takes place after a second civil war in the United States that leaves Manhattan a no man's land. But it is perhaps in France that literature depicting the country's transformation into a patchwork territory has developed the most: this vein began with Jean Raspail's *Camp of the Saints* and continued more recently with Michel Houellebecq's *Submission* and *Les Événements* by Jean Rolin,[12] novels in which a country's fragmentation into armed pockets is always the consequence of a migrant invasion or a civil war in which "hoods" mount attacks against cities.

In short, the undermining of territories also operates in the imaginary, and this imaginary has a performative effect: it further encourages individuals to join virtual communities of people who believe they are alike.

The triumph of subcultures

The concept of subculture originated in the Chicago School (in sociology, not economics), which had studied immigrant groups within American society in the 1920s. In the United Kingdom, Richard Hoggart, the previously cited author of *The Uses of*

Literacy[13] (first published in 1957), his seminal work on the culture of the English working class, founded the Centre for Contemporary Cultural Studies in 1964, where his successor, Stuart Hall, continued to promote "cultural studies" that are the focus of debate today. Since the Chicago School, countless studies have been carried out on subcultures beyond ethnic or racial groups: gangs, youth, occupational groups, companies.[14] It is worth pointing out, however, that the first author to have studied what we would call "black culture" today, William E. B. Du Bois (the first Afro-American to earn a PhD), whose *Souls of Black Folk* was published in 1903, never used the term "black culture," but instead "soul" or "self."[15] He thus referred to an inner life, a worldview, that defines the position of the black person in his/her dialectical relationship with the white society in which he/she lives, without constructing the group of black people as an autonomous category. This approach, which takes personal experience as a starting point, is also found in the work of Albert Memmi[16] and Frantz Fanon.[17] None of these authors took a sociological or anthropological approach, because they were not seeking to give a "positivity" or a content to what shapes the Black or the colonised soul, which they often wrote about in the singular ("the" colonised, "the" American Negro, etc.).

A subculture classically pertains to a group within a dominant culture that brings together people characterised by a set of specific features that are shared, but highly variable from a sociological standpoint (a social class, a particular activity—a corporation, a trade, a company, and so on—the voluntary decision to join a dissident group or gang, an ethnic origin, an age group, a religious practice, a community of tastes or affinities, etc.). These people recognise each other by sharing codes and cultural practices that differentiate them within the dominant culture or set them apart from it (for instance, by using a specific slang or distinguishing features, even negative ones). Countercultures are forms of subculture because they, too, exist only within the framework of a dominant culture. The difference with the anthropological approach to a group within a given society (for instance André Burguière's major study on the Bretons of Plozévet in 1975), is that the latter strives to present the group studied "methodologically as an isolate, with its singularity and its organic unity,"[18] whereas the study of subcultures strives to apprehend them in their relationship to the dominant culture. Cultural studies added another dimension: it placed relations of domination, alienation or on the contrary emancipation at the centre of this relationship.

An authentic culture can very well become a subculture when it is absorbed into another culture that has become dominant: for example, Native Americans on reservations now form communities that are closer to a subculture than to an anthropological culture, because the very ethos of their former culture is no longer tenable (as Lear described in *Radical Hope*); likewise, immigrants in general form subcultures in their host societies rather than real societies. Remarks such as "you'd think we were in Bab el Oued" refer precisely to a culture reduced to segments of culture reconstituted (food, clothing), rather than transplanted.

This is how anthropological culture can be expressed in a "code" culture, because the subculture places more emphasis on collective attitudes highlighted by those involved (celebrations, language, music, dress, etc.) in the framework of a given society than the desire to create a new society.[19] For example, various argots are codes, not languages: *verlan* (back slang) is a coded form of French, not a language that invents itself. In "natural" languages, language precedes grammar; with codes, it is the opposite (the speaker can define the rules of utterance). As subcultures are at once integrated into and distinct from a dominant culture, they usually involve rites of passage that establish the difference between the society and the subgroup (initiation, hazing). Subcultures can exclude; they are hence associated with explicit forms of violence, which are more diffuse in the encompassing society (not necessarily physical violence, as can be seen in the verbal violence of affinity groups on the internet). They thus have explicit codes from the outset (as for example a gang's code of honour). Unlike language, a code is acquired through a learning process that is akin to initiation: to use the code, one must know the rules, whereas it is not necessary to know grammar to speak a language.

Membership of a subculture may be perceived as a matter of either fate or choice. The notions of loyalty and solidarity are associated with membership of the group: we need only read the analyses or narratives by so-called class defectors such as Annie Ernaux, Édouard Louis, or Richard Hoggart to understand how these subcultures weigh on those who are born into them, but also the insecurity of subcultures. For what has gradually disappeared is precisely sociological grounding in some kind of territory. Studies of social group subcultures (trades or working classes) today are tinted with the same nostalgia as those of "primitive societies" once were: the nostalgia of an order and a way of life that no longer exist.

However, as of the second half of the twentieth century, new more fluid subcultures have emerged that no longer fit into easily identifiable sociological categories. They have come together around consumer objects, leisure pursuits, exchanges of ideas or any form of craze (e.g. "fandoms"). Two evolutions affect subcultures: they become autonomous from the dominant culture, whose superiority they reject or ignore, and they become global: whether formed around the Beatles, rap, *Star Wars*, manga, *Lord of the Rings*, *Harry Potter*, yoga, martial arts, the use of emojis or football, subcultures no longer need to be understood within the framework of a dominant culture anchored in a specific place. The crisis of anthropological culture thus "liberates" subcultures, but finally repositions all cultures as subcultures, at least psychologically, because individuals perceive themselves as belonging to a minority or as being "minoritised," and thus retranslate what they believe is their culture into an explicit subculture code. Some today talk about the "dictatorship of the minority," but that is only possible because a majority no longer exists. Sociologists note that we live to some extent in archipelago societies, and those who claim to belong to a majority lament its disappearance, either with nostalgia, or with an apocalyptic sense of "the great replacement."[20]

Clearly the development of the internet has enabled these subcultures to become autonomous, taking shape without being constrained by reality, any form of territoriality or any sociological grounding. But once again, it should be noted that certain keys to the internet culture precede the internet. Take the typical example of youth culture. This is a subculture that became autonomous, whereas by definition and in all societies, young people were grouped together precisely to train them to become adults (the study of "rites of passage" is a requirement in classical anthropological studies): in this regard, hazing, scout induction ceremonies, and military service were all forms of rites of passage.

The autonomy of the globalised youth culture

The notion of a youth culture that is anything other than a transitional moment and an initiation into adult life is a completely new idea in anthropology.

It emerged in the precise sociological context of the construction of "youth" as an autonomous category. Youth is no longer defined as merely the stage preceding adulthood (an anthropological constant) but as a category in itself that has its own resources and is capable of influencing cultural production, even producing the culture it consumes. "Youth" is a construction from the sociological standpoint, as it is experienced in an increasingly loose relationship with the parents' socio-occupational group. The early twentieth century saw the dawn of youth movements (first the scouts, then young Catholic and communist movements, which in their early days were clearly anchored in a specific parental social environment, for instance the Young Christian Workers group and the Catholic Agricultural Youth movement), summer camps and youth literature. In the 1950s, young people started to be autonomous economic actors: they consumed, they influenced the cultural industries market, especially through the music they listened to (the Beatles or dedicated radio programmes such as *Salut les copains*), and spawned a garment economy (brands), all culminating in today's digital social media. May 1968 represented political empowerment: it was the first time that youth formed a movement in itself, rather than simply being the avantgarde of a more encompassing social movement. Today, this autonomy goes a step further: youth culture, deterritorialised by the internet, no longer needs to transit via the adult world, view it as a model or goal, or even stand in opposition to it. One can play the adolescent one's whole life. As will be seen further on, the term "play" should be taken literally: "adults" keep their childhood games or invent new ones.[21]

The most typical case of youth culture autonomy is music. Music knows no language or border; it appeals directly to the body. Note that all conservative criticism, since the advent of jazz, has denounced the "animality" of "young people's" music, of course associated with the real or fantasised fact that it grew out of a "black" world—from jazz to rap and including hiphop. Globalisation is therefore associated (in this case negatively) with deculturation, in other words a state of nature. George Steiner, who bemoaned the death of high culture, noted the emergence of music, as opposed to verbality, as a dominant mode of expression of new cultural forms: "Everywhere a sound-culture seems to be driving back the old authority of the verbal order."[22] This is a profound remark, because globalisation naturally tries to overcome linguistic divides: investment in music (alongside the development of *Globish* English) is an essential vehicle for this transformation. Everywhere, music cultures are being created that instantly go global (rock, hiphop, techno, etc.). This is an entirely new phenomenon, because musical forms have hitherto been borrowed or imported: for instance, Japanese musicians have appropriated the art of playing Bach and Beethoven, but they produce practically no classical music in the Western sense, whereas they make techno and hiphop quite naturally. Allan Bloom denounced this passion for music among young Americans as a prodrome of a disaffection for books: "Nothing is more singular about this generation [of students] than its addiction to music. This is the age of music and the states of soul that accompany it."[23] The development of youth culture is often perceived as an anthropological rupture (a crisis of transmission and imitation) but especially as a delegitimisation of high culture. I will therefore now examine where things stand with high culture, or the cultural canon.

3

CULTURE AS CANON

THE FRAGILITY OF TRANSMISSION

Culture, understood as a corpus, as canon, is a set of products and practices (oral narratives, writings, works—which are then described as artistic—music, even certain forms of ritualised practices) that are selected and taught, in other words handed down according to rules and procedures, with axiological intent, providing a moral ideal for all (the ideal of the Greek *paideia*, the German *Bildung*, the *honnête homme* in seventeenth century France, *adab* in the Muslim world, etc.). Normativity and pedagogy thus go hand in hand: the aim is to define an "ideal," over and above all possible aesthetic forms (including the cynical, the realist, the pessimist and the decadent, all of which can be considered vice's tribute to virtue).

Canonical culture is thus "objectified" as a well-defined ensemble, with associated features: rules for inclusion in the canon (with the age-old conflict between the "ancients" and "moderns"); validation procedures (diplomas, exams, textbooks); places designed for transmitting, establishing, and preserving the canon (universities, museums, theatres, libraries); an associated corps of professionals (mandarins, ulemas, Brahmans, scholars, professors, curators). Producers of the most accomplished and highly respected canonical elements, such as writers and artists, have a legal and fiscal status which in return defines their creations as "artistic." Since the nineteenth century, the artist's legal status in Europe has coincided with the romantic valorisation of the artist as a creative "genius" (the alliance of the attorney and the Muse). Likewise, cultural venues have been established. An object in a museum is a work of art, even if it is a fork. This is how the "primordial arts" (to avoid saying "primitive") were constructed recently at the Quai Branly Museum in Paris: not according to any anthropological criterion, but by our aesthetic view of an object that has been removed from the context of its production and use in the culture where it originated. In short, the work of art is defined by how we view it: for a craftsman in the Middle Ages, a sculpture for a church was not a work of art but the product of an act of worship combined with technical skill, as were the religious cantatas performed today in concert halls rather than in churches. This vision of art as high culture may have been born in the West, but the extension of the museum model, the art market and the "artist" category have made it fully global. This is reflected in the enthusiasm of today's Gulf oil monarchies for the extension of the domain of culture and art (here it is of course more a matter of kitsch than art, but kitsch has become the contemporary form of universal art). During the twentieth century, the particular status of art was called into question in several ways: by the action of the artist, now more important than the work itself (the typical example remains the urinal that Duchamp ironically exhibited in a museum), by regarding everything as art (folk art, *art naïf*, primitive art, design), or by the art market that constructs the value of a work by expanding its audience, for reasons that may be economic or political (the democratisation of culture dear to

the left). In contemporary painting and sculpture, the market
now defines what counts as a work of art: the ranking of artists
(*Kunstkompass*) put out by a well-known trade magazine is based
solely on the number of exhibitions in which they have taken
part.[1] But this evolution is part of a vast trend of "deconstructing" high culture.

The canon thus implies a dimension of legitimacy and/or
legitimation, a criterion of social distinction and a purpose (being
cultured). The canon is always "above" the individual, even above
society. It also marks out a civilisational space, that is, the sphere
of influence of a given high culture, regardless of political territorialisation: Islamic civilisation, Western and Eastern Christianity,
Chinese civilisation and so on. Lastly, the places of cultural production and transmission are not necessarily linked to political
power: madrasas and both Christian and Buddhist monasteries
have created their own spheres of influence, in the form of networks that expand and self-replicate.

One place where high culture is defined and perpetuated is the
university. The modern university emerged in Europe in the
thirteenth century. It gained its autonomy from religion starting
in the sixteenth century, gradually achieving its ideal type: the
nineteenth century German university, constructed around uni-
fying principles of culture and rational critique, with a teaching
faculty taken from its ranks who enjoyed both intellectual and
institutional autonomy. This model spread worldwide to the
detriment of more religious institutions, which have since fallen
back on "pure" religion (madrasas, monasteries). After decoloni-
sation (in which students often played a central role), newly
independent states built upon any existing colonial legacy (the
University of Algiers established by France retained its structure
in independent Algeria) or established their own universities
using the same model. There is thus a historically close link
between university and nation, even if high culture exists in a

sphere extending beyond the national space and universities. Literature of course is created outside universities (few professors are novelists and few good novelists are professors), but it is taught in university and those who might study it outside this framework are called "self-taught," a fairly derogatory term in our contemporary societies.

With university we therefore have a place, a teaching faculty, disciplines, rational production methods, institutional autonomy, degrees, carefully designed curricula and exams based solely on measuring knowledge and merit, providing an education that ensures continuity, reproduction and research and that promotes innovation, secularisation and rational thought. The "hard" sciences are taught alongside the humanities, with bridges between them, because we believe that the purpose of knowledge is to train individuals and further progress.

While the model claims to be universal, universities always develop within a national (but not necessarily state) framework.[2] A university degree is perceived as a requirement to access jobs in the public sector and some in the private sector. The principle is not in dispute: since culture has escaped the control of the Catholic Church, it has developed universities on the model of those of the secular state. Tensions affecting the university for the past century revolve around two questions: social selection (how to open up the ranks of the elite) and state control (French-style state monopoly or US-style private model).

The paradox is that high culture professes to be a monument to civilisation, in other words demonstrating the greatness of the human spirit wherever it may originate, whereas it is underpinned by a nation-building project, in the spirit of the Treaties of Westphalia of 1648, which established the functions of national sovereignty for European states: institutions, remembrance, language, history, and so on. Even music, though free of linguistic constraints, is used in nation-building (Bartók for

Hungary, Sibelius for Finland and even Wagner for Germany). The cultural canon, which grew out of "the classics" (Greek and Latin), remained non-national in Europe as long as it was expressed in Latin. But the emergence of the modern nation-state went hand in hand with the selection of a canon for the national language (which had been codified and standardised), the creation of a new corpus (which might incorporate part of the preceding one), and the construction of a national literature and art. Unlike the universities of the Middle Ages, where teaching was done in Latin, those of the nineteenth century were national universities in terms of language, recruitment, admission into the state apparatus, and even the breakdown of disciplines. Foreign literature is always dealt with in the framework of "comparative literature" and "area studies," usually defined by language (departments of "Romance studies," "Germanic studies," "Scandinavian studies," etc.). Even if a "transnational" canon was maintained, with great names in literature (Shakespeare, Goethe, Hugo, etc.), music and certain disciplines such as philosophy (and later the social sciences), universities remained essentially national until the end of the twentieth century.[3]

The status of high culture is always fragile, because, unlike anthropological culture, it exists only through explicit transmission. It is the very means of such transmission that are being called into question today, by several factors and movements that I will now examine.

The standard globalisation of "mass culture"

High culture was challenged not in relation to political stances on the left or right but in terms of the conflict between humanism and anti-humanism, or the critique of humanism.

The first shot was fired by the Frankfurt School in 1947: Horkheimer and Adorno, exiled to the United States, critiqued what they called "the culture industry." In the 1950s, this condemnation of what came to be called "mass culture" was taken up by both conservatives (T. S. Eliot) and radical progressives (Guy Debord). Mass culture is not the same as "popular" culture. It is the product of an economic system and aims to cut through class lines: it comes from on high, and so is not comparable to the various subcultures that came to the fore in the 1960s, such as underground culture and the cultures associated with music trends. It was a new concept. As Christopher Lasch noted, following Adorno, mass culture destroys both popular culture and high culture.[4] It is a decontextualised, dehistoricised consumer culture, enabled by techniques of sound and image reproduction, and accessible to all with no prior instruction owing to new, inexpensive means of production and circulation (paperbacks, records, movies, radio, television, cartoons). Both the conservative right and the progressive left viewed the development of mass culture as having an alienating and numbing effect on the human mind. The former placed more stress on the need to preserve high culture in a generally elitist manner,[5] while the latter called for the popularisation of the existing high culture and the expansion of cultural spaces accessible to the people (ranging from the Bolshoi Theatre in the Soviet Union to Jean Vilar's *Théâtre populaire* in France, as well as the establishment of *Maisons de la culture* under André Malraux's culture ministry).

Mass culture also paved the way for globalisation by bringing standardised products onto the market. The Disney productions of the 1930s (*Snow White and the Seven Dwarfs*, the first Disney film, dates back to 1937) easily overcame cultural barriers, as did later television series, of which *Dallas* (1978) was the archetype. If there is a close relationship between mass culture and deculturation, it is less due to the working class becoming consumers of culture (which is what conservatives frown on) than to the capacity of mass culture to become deterritorialised and to circulate from one culture to another. Disney launched this patchwork culture by borrowing elements from fairy tales (Snow White) and history (Robin Hood) and "remixing" them in a sugar-coated format.[6] In this regard, and despite a lack of deliberate strategy, the development of the entertainment industry paved the way for the worldwide spread of a culture in kit form accessible to all. Mass culture is perfectly compatible with the globalisation of culture because it brought about its decontextualisation.

Yet such products were not designed to go global: in the 1950s, the American entertainment industry took little interest in export and its production was solely for the American market. When these productions came to Europe, they were perceived as partaking in the Americanisation of ways of life, along with CocaCola and later McDonald's (both of which soon developed an export policy). This explains the illusion that mass culture is an American culture; but it does not help explain why it spread throughout the world, among diverse populations that easily adopted it despite the objections of cultural elites and an activist left, as shown by the regular attacks on McDonald's franchises in France.

In the space created by mass culture, new objects would soon start to circulate that were produced and consumed in the framework of the "youth culture" described in Chapter 2. Even if they have been seized upon by an entertainment economy (producers of cartoons and films, impresarios for up-and-coming singers, etc.) that is prepared to make money from anything that circulates, these objects were launched "from below": they often begin circulating underground, or among fringe fandoms, or through artisanal low-budget productions, before entering sooner or later into a closer relationship with the entertainment industry, which exploits trends and tastes more than it initiates them.

The autonomisation of youth is a fundamental phenomenon and I again emphasise the fact with respect to the crisis of high culture, because it weakens the necessary chain of transmission. Cultural transmission now has trouble functioning from the top down; it is instead conceived of only horizontally, among "peers," even among the like-minded. This crisis of transmission is at the core of the deculturation I am trying to understand, affecting anthropological culture and the cultural canon alike.

This generational decentring has been compounded more recently by a geographical decentring. "Cultures" other than American are putting products on the market that circulate worldwide. The best example of this is Japanese manga. How could a specific, self-referential culture like that of Japan produce for export, particularly as a manga is not a Honda? At a less universal level, we can think of Brazilian *telenovelas*, Turkish television series and Bollywood movies. The reason is simple: this McDonald's culture was no longer based on historic cultures but rather prefigured what would become global culture at the end of the twentieth century. I will return to this question, but the initial "operation" is to "sequence" fragments of culture (in both senses of the term) and to uproot them from their home soil, which makes them highly mobile because they are decontextualised. If need be, advertising scenarios invent a new euphoric environment for them (image of happiness, standardisation of emotions). This emergence of a new global mass culture is neither a consequence nor a cause of the crisis of high culture, with which it has an ambiguous relationship, as will be seen. It occurs at one remove from high culture.

The humanities as imposture

Alongside being outflanked by new, global cultures and their fandoms, high culture is experiencing an internal crisis. As Bill Readings has pointed out, cultural studies are not the cause but rather the consequence of the crisis of culture (just as same-sex marriage is not the cause but the consequence of the crisis of the family model):

> It is no accident that at this point a number of transdisciplinary movements arise that pose the question of identity otherwise: Women's Studies, Lesbian and Gay Studies, Postcolonial Studies, and Cultural Studies. Such movements signal the end of the reign of literary culture as the organizing discipline of the University's cultural mission, for they loosen the tie between the subject and the nation-state. The emergence of critical practices that question the status of the literary and pay attention to popular culture is not the cause of the decline of literature, but its effect.[7]

The crisis of high culture is being played out first of all in universities, which is only to be expected. The university system is the quintessential place where the cultural canon is processed and reproduced. In France, the alarmist discourse of "declining standards" became more structured as of the 1960s as education became more widespread, to the point where 80% of school students were sitting the baccalaureate and shortly after that going on to institutions of higher education. Greek and Latin are still taught, and an American student may still write a thesis on the *Chanson de Roland*, but as Allan Bloom remarks, "Classical music is now a special taste, like Greek language or pre-Columbian archaeology, not a common culture of reciprocal communication and psychological shorthand."[8] Nor is it any accident that the university is the main battlefield for the "war of values" that we find ourselves in: from Trump's America to antiwoke France, the university is accused of being the place where the humanities and national culture are betrayed. The big problem with conservatives is that they do not understand the university crisis: for them it is rooted in the subversion of its purpose by "enemies" from poor neighbourhoods, from overseas, from the fringes or from within, rather than in a crisis internal to the notion of high culture itself. This problem is the "barbarians" (Bloom goes so far as to call the students themselves "natives," an attitude later echoed in France with the emergence of the *"Indigènes de la République"* post-colonialist, anti-racist movement and party):

> But in 1960, inasmuch as most of most of intellectual life had long ago settled in universities and the American ones were the best, their decay or collapse was a catastrophe. Much of the great tradition was here, an alien and weak transplant, perched precariously in enclaves, vulnerable to native populism and vulgarity. In the mid-sixties the natives, in the guise of students, attacked.[9]

Attacks on culture are thus vilified for being driven by the pernicious influence of new schools of thought that have grown out of the deconstruction championed by French theory, postcolonial and cultural studies, ideologies (wokeism) or teaching methods: this is the conservative lament regarding the expansion of relativism, the end of the pre-eminence of high literature (great books and great authors) in favour of the sanctification of the trivial and the commonplace.[10] Faced with the various challenges to high culture, the "Ancients" have retreated into handwringing and advocate the return to authoritarian pedagogy, in other words, a culture that is precisely disconnected from contemporary society (hence life). In this regard the discourse of these "Ancients" against the new "Moderns" is deeply pessimistic. They have shifted to the right, even the extreme right, because they have given up on modernity in all its forms. But conservatives seem to forget that the German university model discussed above, so admired by Bloom and Readings and copied to some extent by France after the defeat of 1870, also produced and promoted Nazism. As Christian Baechler points out in *La Trahison des élites allemandes,* "Support for Hitler rose with educational level," which is problematic if we want to pursue a link between university and civilisation.[11] Nazism is probably the greatest symptom of the crisis of Western culture, and its expansion was made possible due to the support of its elites. Conservatives today would do well to remember that.

* * *

Critiques of high culture as they were formulated by the traditional university are sustained by currents that constantly hurl abuse at one another while hastening its deconstruction. Among them I see several major inspirations: neoliberalism (for which high culture allegedly serves no purpose, nor does the notion of a person's moral and intellectual training), a critique of the nation-state (the canon is first and foremost "national" and has trouble withstanding globalisation) and cultural and postcolonial studies (that claim that the corpus alienates rather than liberates), not to forget religious fundamentalism, in particular the American Protestant variety. Newly founded universities in this vein, such as Liberty University in Lynchburg, Virginia, have virtually eliminated the teaching of the humanities in favour of theology, law and communication.

The radical left sees high culture as socially discriminating, a sign of affiliation with an elite that is given an education for the sole purposes of legitimizing its domination (especially that of the "white" world) and social control. Deconstructing means unmasking the pretension to universality of a culture that remains deeply ideological, as it leads the dominated to accept their own alienation. This is not a new idea: it was present in Marxism, in Nietzsche's call to overturn values and to a certain extent in psychoanalysis, which attempts to detect unconscious desire and the role of repression, in other words the illusion behind all moral constructs. It became the common denominator of Derrida's deconstruction philosophy, postcolonial studies inspired by Edward Saïd's critique of orientalism and Bourdieu's sociology. My aim here is not to go into the bases for these theories or to examine their merits. We can readily acknowledge that high culture at once conceals and reveals, essentialises even as it analyses, justifies the particular by reference to the universal, euphemises the violence of deculturation and is in no way a guarantee of peace, tolerance and truth. Hence there can be no living high culture without criticism, debate and opposition. Nevertheless, deconstruction does not in itself bring about liberation, and the idea of high culture itself—as opposed to a given literary or philosophical corpus—cannot be jettisoned just like that. The question is therefore to know how criticism, which is legitimate in itself, can lead to a normative system, the consequence of which is the levelling of the very concept of culture.

Neoliberal excellence

If cultural studies critiques and neoliberalism both perceive high culture as a form of imposture, it would be an error to view challenges to it as a conflict between right and left. Defence of the humanities also comes from the left (Lasch, Michéa and even Bloom refuse to be pigeonholed on the right in this regard), whereas a segment of the neoliberal right relishes the destruction of the university that emerged in the nineteenth century (Margaret Thatcher did her best to undermine the system). In France, the merger of classical and modern courses of study (schematically, the middle class and the working class) as well as the gradual marginalisation of Latin, deemed elitist, was implemented by the right in the 1960s and 70s.[12] The disappearance of Latin is of course related to a change in the notion of what culture is: up until the late nineteenth century, Latin gave access to a corpus considered to be a source of moral and political inspiration. Having been central to the civilisational ethos, it then became simply a marker of membership in the elite (the best students studied Latin), after which, when other more useful and functional markers fulfilled this role, it was relegated to being one option among many.[13]

The radical critique from the left paradoxically combines with the injunctions of neoliberalism, which find expression in the current theory of excellence applied to the university: the "Shanghai criteria" which have been internationally recognised since 2003. These involve defining a sort of excellence that is totally removed from local cultures in order to compare universities throughout the world. The difference with the university model established in the nineteenth century is considerable: the excellence thus evaluated is no longer the consummate ideal of a given culture, in this case that of the West; it can only be defined by avoiding any precise cultural reference. For comparison to be possible, the comparative evaluation of universities presupposes that all cultural references be removed. This implies the end of the humanities, historical grounding and the imaginary of an ethos, in other words the moral purpose of education.

Excellence must also be amenable to quantitative measurement. But general culture is by definition unquantifiable, because it does not lead to practical skills. One might remember how former French president Sarkozy expressed surprise that *La Princesse de Clèves*, a great seventeenth-century literary classic, was on the curriculum for the competitive exam for administrative officers.[14] What he was attacking, beyond a canon that was perhaps rather outmoded, was the very ethos that high culture claimed to instil. Neither the people nor the new elites have need of this ethos (and this is a point of divergence between neoliberals and conservatives). High culture is either a waste of time or one hobby among many. General education is thus replaced by an à la carte system of segments of knowledge, with no reference to a whole. But what was fundamental in high culture, even when it was demoted to general culture, is that it was the expression of a whole, a system of references shared by all, whatever

61

their occupation, age or prior education. Everyone, or at least every member of the elite, had to share a common body of knowledge and references, roughly equating to what students were expected to learn in secondary school before specializing in a course of study at university. This is what is destroyed by the à la carte educational system, now recommended as early as secondary school in France.[15] We have gone from a common body of knowledge to a catalogue of courses for all tastes. Latin, guitar, film studies and Chinese are all interchangeable options. I am not criticizing the right to choose; I simply take issue with the disappearance of a certain architecture of knowledge.

Take for example a key principle in the neoliberal quest for excellence: the theory of benchmarking, which involves adopting the best practices or technique observed in the competition in order to standardise practices and performance with respect to a common measure.[16] It therefore implies deculturating a practice. Imagine we find an innovative sales, production or management technique in the United States or China. We're obviously not going to study Chinese, American or Japanese culture before imitating it. We will lift the interesting segment out of its cultural context and integrate it into our own practice. The sequencing and grafting of "good practice" is somewhat akin to genome sequencing: management engineering mirrors biological engineering.[17]

This strategy of excellence has two fundamental consequences in relation to culture: it disregards both anthropological culture and high culture. From the standpoint of anthropological culture, borrowing a "good practice" certainly does not amount to understanding the cultural context that enabled it, for that would make it conceptually impossible to extract it from its context and transpose it elsewhere. Therein lies all the tension that runs through management experts and the world of work. On one hand, people are prepared to take a culturalist approach: there have long been discussions about the Japanese work culture, cultural obstacles to development,[18] the need to consider national cultures or company cultures in developing one's activity and getting the best out of one's managers. Countless cultural awareness seminars are organised to learn how to negotiate in China. But on the other hand, little notice is taken of these lessons, which are more of a box-ticking exercise than a rationalisation of management practices. Management training seminars for managers, usually in an idyllic setting of a sunny resort, are highly popular, but quality control practices totally disregard the cultural dimension (and, let's be honest, the human dimension as well, as these practices never approach individuals holistically, in their relationship to the world, which is precisely the field of culture). Professional activity is chopped up into discontinuous sequences that are each subject to quantified assessment according to a pre-established grid, with the aim to standardise and equalise work practices and actions. Deculturation thus ends with dehumanisation.[19]

If the theory of excellence entirely fails to take high culture into account, it is precisely because high culture cannot be sequenced without being adulterated, because it remains deeply rooted in national cultural, or at least linguistic, spaces. A book, written by an influential British education secretary that claims to be the textbook for excellence in schools, never mentions culture as a criterion except as an allusion to hobbies: "good schools [...] make substantial provision for extra-curricular activities including sports, the arts, voluntary activities and other after-school activities," all other criteria of excellence are purely functional (teacher/student ratio, the role of parents and, always, the emphasis on personal achievement).[20]

Adherence to the Shanghai criteria has led universities to self-deculturate with the blessing of right-wing governments. A nation's culture now boils down to heritage, remembrance, tradition and conservation—in other words a museum. Literature is no longer taught as canon but as a juxtaposition of segments of thematic writings, with no historical contextualisation. The spread of English moreover is leading to the emergence of a field of global knowledge (with professor mobility and untethered places of education and debate) and the provincialisation of fields that are not translated or rarely translated.

Horizontal knowledge

The university is no longer the primary avenue for access to knowledge. The opposition between "scholar" and "autodidact," a foundational element in the establishment of universities (this opposition did not exist until the nineteenth century), makes less and less sense. The self-taught have evened the score: they plug any query into Google and then possess the knowledge they sought. But while they can claim to know, they can also find countless scholars who in turn criticise "official" knowledge. There is no longer any academic consensus on how to define a scientist, as the controversies surrounding Covid19 demonstrated: the boundary between charlatan and scientist has become blurred.[21] It is of course likely that consensus on scientific truth has never existed, but owing to a corporatist, even unionist reflex, debate took place mainly within the university. Hoaxes, plagiarism, ideological extrapolation and bias have always been part of the history of science. But at least the university could speak in the name of knowledge when it was addressing the layperson.

The very configuration of knowledge has changed. This is true above all of data collection both on the quantitative level (an extraordinary amount of information can be gathered by combing the internet) and the qualitative level (for everything depends on what one considers an objective "fact"). This instant availability of information appears to be a huge step forward, but it contains its own limits; the information gathered is never raw data, of the kind a researcher can use for analysis using a neutral, explicit and objective methodology. This mass of data, i.e. big data, can only be sorted and processed by complex algorithmic systems that nevertheless produce an immediate result: through a combination of statistical correlations that involve both large data sets (written texts) and very small data (traces of internet searches, counts of clicks and likes), it produces a set of responses treated, without any methodology, as if they were pieces of objective knowledge. As Dominique Cardon says, "While public discourse today focuses on the extravagant volume of digital data and the threats that mining it poses to individual privacy, the main challenge facing big data is to make sense of this maelstrom of raw data."[22] Algorithms function solely by comparing big data sets from a strictly statistical standpoint: they pay no heed to genealogies of meaning, to cultural allusions or to past history. They do not perform an archaeology of knowledge as discussed by Foucault. The data retrieved is flat, without depth or perspective, and its significance is merely statistical: authors who are cited frequently are necessarily "good" or, more precisely, their worth is based solely on the statistical frequency of their mention.

Knowledge is no longer a corpus that is the product of a history (of history generally speaking, epistemology, the history of science, the context in which discoveries were made, etc.). Knowledge is "flattened" because it is cut off from its own history. It refers only to itself. "Deep knowledge" is self-referential.

As Yoshua Bengio aptly sums it up:

Here's how it works: for a computer to become intelligent, we have to enable it to acquire knowledge through observation of examples and interaction with its environment. Classic methods of directly giving the computer knowledge, like writing formulas in a book or programming a computer the usual way, are reversed. In machine learning, on the contrary, we look at the knowledge the computer has acquired. It's important, because much of human knowledge is not accessible to our intellect, in particular things that are intuitive, and we don't know how to program a computer so that this knowledge, which is obvious to us, or intuitive, precisely because we can't break it down, analyse it, put it in words... But sometimes, even often, to translate something properly, it is also necessary to understand what the language is referring to. And there is the rub, because language only enables us to convey certain information; everything that falls under what we call common sense or intuition cannot be conveyed and in fact we have no need to, but it is necessary to understand the sentences. Computers have a real lack of the rich and intuitive understanding of the world around us and that they will need to reach human-level intelligence.[23]

The host of archives that exist in the Web, the count of clicks, likes, purchases and internet searches make it possible to set up a statistical apparatus that does not need to analyse the social profile of actors. These are reduced to specific actions, to segments of behaviour that disregard motivation, the unconscious, culture and sociological background. Surveys and polls are therefore self-referential (as is software measuring radicalisation or delinquency).[24] Actors are no longer apprehended in terms of their social existence: "Rejecting inherited and statutory positions, [this technique of calculation] aggregates reputation by assessing activities independently of places occupied in society."[25]

Consequently, this type of research can dispense with the human sciences because it no longer needs a theoretical apparatus. It is enough, at least on the surface, to observe correlations and regard them as constants. In Dominique Cardon's analysis,

Correlation is not causation. In an article that caused quite a stir, Chris Anderson, a Silicon Valley guru, announced 'the end of theory.' Computer clusters analysing big data, he explained, can now look for correlations without a model to explain them. Massive amounts of data and applied mathematics will make the scientific method obsolete.[26]

The "human" sciences therefore no longer have a role to play, because there is no longer any need to seek the meaning of actions, to examine what is unsaid or implicit and even less to think in terms of values. This perhaps explains the expansion of quantitative research in sociology and even in political science, to the detriment of qualitative research based on discussion and interaction with the research subjects. We now have to struggle to keep up with the machine. But as these new human sciences always lag behind mathematical knowledge, the development of algorithms and research conducted by the tech giants, their dehumanisation does not make them more scientific, it simply makes them disappear. This time by suicide. The university crisis is also a crisis in our relationship to knowledge.

A radical critique would simply recommend discarding high culture altogether, the problem being not so much access to high culture but its very nature: its content can be viewed as a factor of ideological control and therefore of either class or imperialist alienation. By claiming to be above classes, it allegedly prevents dominated groups from attaining the universal, because they do not identify with it and their "lack of culture" is thrown back in their faces. This means that it is not only the content of high culture that is problematic, but the idea of high culture itself. Culture is the enemy. Rather than opening museums to the people, they must be closed. This trend is not specific to the West. The Chinese Cultural Revolution attacked classical culture head-on: the last campaign of the Cultural Revolution in 1974, "criticise Lin (Piao) (likely successor of Mao Zedong), criticise Confucius" (pī Lín pī Kǒng), aimed to make a clean sweep of classical Chinese culture and moreover had detrimental effects on libraries and works of art. The rehabilitation of Confucianism by subsequent regimes mainly involved reducing it to a normative system of social behaviour and political conformism, in other words a de facto confirmation of the conversion of traditional culture into a code. In the contemporary Muslim world, Salafis have also rejected traditional culture, literature, *adab*, poetry, philosophy, *falsafa* and music, in various, sometimes violent ways, including the exclusion of anything to do with philosophy and literature from the curricula, and fatwas urging not only the avoidance of profane culture, but also the destruction of musical instruments, books and mosques not to their liking.[27]

But such a position is untenable: it presupposes either the return to a tabula rasa through revolution, which would necessarily be violent, or the self-ghettoisation of a group closed in on itself, which is then under constant pressure from the encompassing society. We cannot live without culture. We cannot live without an imaginary. The crisis in the loci of production of high culture does not mean the end of cultural consumption.

So what remains of what we call "culture"?

4

THE CRISIS OF IMAGINARIES

Every culture reflects an imaginary, a belief system that not only gives it meaning, but enables the meaning to take root and be shared. The imaginary is thus also "believing". Michel de Certeau fully grasped what is at issue. In "The Weakness of Believing," he shows how religious faith, organised by the ecclesial institution and rooted in tradition, developed in a shared religious imaginary. But the institutional crisis and the critique of tradition that accompanied Vatican II have rendered faith unstable, floating and unmoored. Such uncertainty has allowed new spiritualities to emerge that have turned their backs on history, the institution and even language, in favour of pathos, suffering and ecstatic subjectivity. According to Certeau, the glossolalia (speaking in tongues) of the new charismatic groups, and in particular the Pentecostals, "brings with it a similar hollowing out of objective contents and the same absence of referent." He goes on:

> The signifiers disappear from the discourse, which is transformed into singing and moaning, pure voice in the ecstasy and fervour of saying oneself in the vanishing of sense. There is an erosion of state-

ment by utterance... [The subject] reappears in the form of a pathos, necessarily a stranger to systems of statements.[1]

Certeau here is of course talking about Christianity in the early 1960s, but as he himself points out, our society remains, or did up until this period at least, in the shadow of Christianity.[2] The crisis of religion mirrors the crisis of culture in general.

* * *

Neither high culture nor anthropological culture provide the stuff of dreams today. "Ways of believing" now come within the realm of subcultures; they are associated with sects, fandoms, conspiracy theories and the like. The end of grand ideologies has also been a defeat for the imagination, just as secularisation has been, as it leaves no other foundation for the political order than a theory of the social contract at odds with everyday experience. Secularism in the nineteenth century claimed to be as much a form of spirituality as an ode to rationality and science (a synthesis central to the tenets of Freemasonry): today it is no more than a normative code that cannot provide an alternative to religious drifts other than to exclude religion. Imaginaries are thus relegated to the margins of societies, leaving the grand narratives in the hands of radicals—the example of the bellicose reinterpretation of jihad being the most striking. Without a common imaginary, it is hard to project oneself into the future: for the first time, a cause mobilising youth (the fight against climate change) is driven not by hope but by fear. It is not a utopia but a nostalgia: for the Earth before the advent of *homo sapiens*.

Kitsch in kit form

The erasure of a shared "cultured" imaginary does not erase the need for imaginaries but shifts it onto decultured products that still fire the imagination: new imaginary spaces unfold in universes created by the culture industry, such as manga, *Game of Thrones*, *Harry Potter* and Marvel Comics. These worlds are all based on a patchwork of cultural borrowings removed from their context (Athena in manga, the feudal knight against the Buddhist karateka, the Middle Ages in science fiction),[3] and on scraps of places, periods and historical figures that are all decontextualised, unmoored, and that can "speak" to everyone. Globalised culture is by definition a kitsch culture.[4] These mashups open up a new, alternative, "uchronic" imaginary space that is atemporal and deterritorialised.

One might object that Japanese manga, which are the epitome of this atemporal imaginary, basically belong to a youth culture. But that is exactly the point: one of the characteristics of youth culture since around the 1960s is that it grows up with the child, so to speak: each new generation (babyboomers, generations X, Y and Z) seem to remain attached to their own youth. The cult of youth does not mean aligning oneself with the most recent generation (defined by its relationship to new technologies and the development of the internet) but perpetuating one's own youth. Youth has become a value in and of itself, something to be preserved. This underlies the trend of delaying parenthood, the portrayal of dashing, athletic seniors, as well as "youthful" pursuits, particularly games, which continue into an advanced age: paintball for managers, role play, video games, battle reenactments, and so on. Adults continue to consume what they watched or listened to as teenagers. Games bring together the three key elements of the present analysis: codes, norms and deculturation. Codes, because everything is explicit on the basis of a finite number of elements (which can be as simple as the six sides of a die, a deck of cards or a much more complex ensemble). It is a system of norms: the game is played by a set of rules and there are sanctions. Lastly, while elements from various cultural origins are used, no cultural context is required to play the game. One cannot appeal to implicit elements not specified by the rules. As Graeber explains, "games are pure rule-governed action."[5] Games have been globalised since Antiquity with very minor variations (the rook, the elephant gambit, the bishop in chess) that change nothing in substance. What is new is the extension of the field of games to spheres of activity such as professional life, psychiatry and even theory. Game theory is not just another framework of analysis among others. It also presupposes (rightly or wrongly) that the agents of an action are rational players who play according to shared rules with no relation to a given culture or cast of mind. The game is a complete sequence with a beginning and an end: it has no context.

Fiction is by definition central to the cultural imaginary. We need only look at the makeup of the fiction corpus, with a circulation far more active than that of literature. What "makes" fiction today is a collage of disparate historical elements: the Middle Ages and Antiquity combined with science fiction (*Game of Thrones, Dungeons & Dragons*). Fantasy triumphs. Even speculative fiction is no longer a projection into the future; it is already here in the present or through a return to the past to change the future, as in the *Terminator* saga. This blend of temporalities destroys the very notion of chronology. Rather than the past explaining the present, history is becoming a mere repertory of exploitable sequences. Today, it is *Dungeons & Dragons*, tomorrow it will be something else, but we live in a permanent atemporal dystopia, even in an ectopia: things are extracted from their "natural environment" and transplanted to places they have no connection with—the Bavarian or Scottish castle plopped down anywhere, a Venetian canal with its Bridge of Sighs and gondolas reproduced in Doha or a Chinese province, not to mention Disneyland. We are in an eternal present, a constant re-creation.

It is of course not new for objects from one culture to circulate in another: jazz and the blues were appropriated by the dominant culture, the court of Louis XIV had a fondness for *Turqueries*, and the discipline known as comparative literature hunts for borrowings, influences and the movement of themes from one culture to another. What is new is the lack of acculturation, in other words, the fact that these elements are not integrated into another culture. They circulate unaltered in very different spaces and therefore form a virtual space untethered to real societies.[6] Earlier manifestations of this manner of subverting reality can be found in the Surrealists' art of collage (the detachment of objects from reality by placing them in a random arrangement was an assertion of the autonomy of meaning), then in Malraux's *Museum Without Walls*,[7] and more recently in the "tribal arts" presented outside of their anthropological context (a precondition, as we have seen, for their access to the status of works of art). The anthropologist James Clifford picked up on this trend very early on:

> The surrealists frequented the Marché aux Puces, the vast flea market of Paris, where one could rediscover the artefacts of culture, scrambled and rearranged. With luck one could bring home some bizarre or unexpected object, a work of art with nowhere to go—'ready-mades' such as Marcel Duchamp's bottle rack, and *objets sauvages*, African or Oceanian sculptures. These objects—stripped of their functional context—were necessary furnishings for the avant-garde studio.[8]

Clifford clearly perceived in the flea market the prototype of what would transform authentic cultures into collections of folkloric gadgets.

Owing to the internet and new means of dissemination, we now have an infinite reservoir of references, cultural segments torn from any original culture, from which we can pick and choose to construct a new assemblage, as if with Lego. World cuisine, playlists, comic books, fashion: everything is patchwork. The musicologist Jean During aptly described this phenomenon with respect to music:

THE CRISIS OF CULTURE

The distinctive characteristic of our time is that everything can be preserved, and this is done almost systematically, through huge excavation sites to collect, catalogue and restore, and this, well beyond the public's expectations and their capacity for reception. Given the mass of available data and the limitless possibilities of reproduction and dissemination, the public can no longer find their references, particularly as, considering all cultures to be equal, the greatest variety of musical forms are all put on the same plane. In any event, if music lovers have the feeling they have access to all of them, they still need to be aware that these are disincarnate and decontextualized acoustic traces that can hardly convey the experience in which they are rooted.[9]

But decontextualisation is precisely what is appealing. It is not perceived as a drawback or as something lacking, but on the contrary a condition for freedom and even self-expression. A playlist brings together songs or pieces that have no relation between them other than the musical taste of the person who compiled it. The use of synthesisers makes it possible to circulate rhythmic music segments attributed to a "culture" (Caribbean, African) but used in entirely different contexts. Consequently, what circulates is a sort of rhythmic cliché. The already ancient history of the "Lambada" (1989), which travelled the globe, is a good example of such circulation of musical clichés associated with an "indigenous" culture that travel out of context.[10] The producers of the video clip that was a summertime hit had adapted the traditional Brazilian rhythms of the dance to a song plagiarised from a Bolivian group, which was then picked up the world over in different languages and with different lyrics.

Such decontextualisation of elements subsequently recomposed—which enables a segment to circulate untethered in random contexts, revamped depending on each person's fantasy and pleasure—is also characteristic of the use of "memes," vignettes (short scene, figure, object) that are stuck at random in different

74

contexts: "With memes, there is at once a decontextualisation of the image, a suppression of the conditions in which it was initially produced and a recontextualisation that gives it new meaning."[11] This is also an apt description of the three stages of construction of a new globalised cultural space.

Cuisine, tourism, religion: a giant patchwork

Cuisine may be the field in which this cultural game of Lego is the most flagrant: Hawaiian pizza, Sicilian tempura,[12] Burgundian couscous, Normandy-style pirojki, furikake masala,[13] etc. Various elements from different cuisines are taken and recomposed to make what is known as fusion food. Added to this table of elements are complex nomenclatures pertaining to the presence or lack of allergens, the number of calories, the nutrient composition in terms of carbohydrates, fat and protein, and so on. Basic foods are thus broken down into categories that are all codified and standardised (in terms of health, even culture: tolerance and harmony, as in the presentation of furikake masala). The increase in cultural tolerance (China and Japan reconciled at the tips of chopsticks) goes hand in hand with growing intolerance to an increasing number of allergens or foodstuffs that are too "something" (fat, sweet, artificial, meaty, etc.). The "food" column in the media no longer targets possible "homemakers"; it no longer publishes recipes and methods reserved for specific users and occasions, but promotes a way of spicing up life. Yet the diversity of references conceals a uniformisation of tastes. This is a trend found for instance in wine, in which the Robert Parker norms (very oaky red wines) has long prevailed, as lamented by filmmaker Jonathan Nossiter in the documentary *Mondovino*.[14] The uniformisation of taste is offset by inflated descriptions of a bottle of wine or a dish, thus ensuring a purely virtual diversity against a backdrop of conformism.

Discourse on food has thus replaced food. It has become impossible to eat without talking about what one is eating, without reading what one is eating, without photographing what one is eating, without sharing images. "Food must be beautiful to be loved," declared Peter Wells, the *New York Times* food critic, worrying that "the good old grilled steak will ultimately disappear from menus because brown is not photogenic."[15] Menus, especially in the United States, have experienced an inflation in adjectives, each creamier and tastier than the next. And it works: a study was conducted at Ithaca College to observe the choices made by a panel of customers in relation to the same dish presented differently on menus. Asked to choose either a concise description and modest price ("An oven-roasted, stuffed, boneless, skinless chicken breast. Served with wild rice and vegetables"), or grandiloquence and a high price ("Citrus marinated chicken breast stuffed under the skin with shrimp and crabmeat, grilled over a hickory fire, then served with a sweet and spicy Georgia peach sauce, saffron wild rice, and fresh vegetables"), customers chose the more sophisticated (and consequently more expensive) menu item, even though the food on the plate was identical in every way.[16]

In short, culinary culture is no longer acquired through the eating experience. The menu does more than describe a dish, it describes the taste of the dish or the wine (creamy, juicy, tasty—which is the least one might expect—with raspberry notes and tannins for wine). The result is not only to render taste, smell and flavour explicit, but also to prescribe taste; a person who cannot detect hints of raspberry in his or her Burgundy is deemed to be an oaf or a curmudgeon. As always, rendering something explicit quickly deviates toward the normative and the recipe turns into a prescription, almost in the medical sense.[17]

This distancing from the sensory experience is also found in tourism. Travel has the purpose not just of learning about a country but of "consuming" what a guide recommends seeing. There again, segments of culture are consumed without any interest in their context. Visitors will throng to "do" the Louvre in Paris or the Uffizi Gallery in Florence to be able to say they have seen the *Mona Lisa* or *The Birth of Venus*. Mario Vargas Llosa, one of the great fault-finders with the crisis of high culture, describes the way people snack or "nibble" on culture:

> These tourist visits 'on the lookout for distractions' undermine the real significance of these museums and monuments, putting them on the same level as other obligations of the perfect tourist: eating pasta and dancing a tarantella in Italy, applauding flamenco and *cante jondo* in Andalucía, and tasting *escargots*, visiting the Louvre and the Folies-Bergère in Paris.[18]

Not even religions escape the benchmarking of practices. The process of sequencing and transposing culturally heterogeneous elements into a repertoire for personal use (in order to "feel good") has for instance been applied to the field of religious feeling: "Evan Sharp, the co-founder of Pinterest, hired Sacred Design Lab to categorize all major religious practices and think of ways to apply them to the office. They made him a spreadsheet [in which they] pulled together hundreds of practices [...] and tried to categorize them by emotional state," which they could refer to the way one would take a pill, smoke a joint or reach for a glass of whisky.[19]

A recurrent debate among sociologists of religion has to do with the relationship between culture and religion among evangelical missionaries from the United States. To my mind, they are at once the product and agents of deculturation. For others, they adapt to local cultures.[20] But all depends on what we mean by culture: missionaries take issue with the anthropological foundation of the society in which they preach (sexual morality, relations between the sexes, leadership), but they borrow segments of local culture (dress, musical instruments). Preaching Jesus in Mexico in a sombrero with mariachis is not cultural adaptation: it is precisely to use culture as folklore, because it involves removing a few segments and making them autonomous, then reinserting them in a totally different context.[21]

Indigenous culture: from anthropology to folklore

Conservatives and progressives alike put up resistance to deculturation, paradoxically in very similar ways. In both cases, the aim is to preserve a heritage that guarantees the identity of a culture. "Left-wing" multiculturalism and the defence of heritage by "right-wing" conservatives follow the same approach. What changes is the heritage to which each refers. The former want to safeguard cultures dominated by "white" Western hegemony and the latter want to shield this Western culture both from hybridisation and from being levelled out.

The paradox is that the forms of resistance to deculturation operate using the same process of sequencing segments into autonomous elements that can circulate untethered. The heritage that one chooses to defend dissolves in its own museumification or folklorisation. However, both multiculturalists and conservatives dream of policies in which the law would require stakeholders to submit to their vision of culture, essentially through censorship (by practising so-called cancel culture or by censoring its practice). The United States today is a remarkable cultural laboratory where Democratic- and Republican-ruled states can be seen to adopt these twin forms of censorship and normative precepts—in both cases, the other is the target. Norms are always the first response from both the right and the left to a culture in crisis; they are not the stuff of dreams, and generating dreams is the function of any culture.

We have seen how subcultures gain autonomy. Multiculturalism values two types of subcultures: "indigenous" cultures and "immigrant" cultures. The name of a movement like *Indigènes de la République* clearly affirms a continuity between the two, not only in demographic terms (although the "racialised" are not always descended from natives of the former colonies), but with regard to the subordinate relationship between the dominant culture, however postcolonial it may be, and dominated cultures, which are defined less by a return to precolonial traditions than by a claim to new identity markers within the dominant culture (an example being the Muslim headscarf, which, as we know, no longer has anything traditional about it either in appearance or in the social function it fulfils when it is worn by university-educated women living in the West). Authenticity does not refer to an anthropological culture that preceded colonisation, but to a desire to assert oneself in a postcolonial framework. "Authentic" cultures have undergone the same simplification and objectivisation process, as observed by anthropologists, and which falls into the well-known category of folklorisation.

Folklore emerged in the late nineteenth century as a by-product of anthropological approaches applied to European rural societies at a time when they were on the verge of disappearing. There is hence no urban folklore (but there are subcultures).[22] "Indigenous" cultures joined them later in the living museums constituted by dance, music and sacred art festivals that have proliferated since the 1980s, in which bits and pieces of different cultures that supposedly resonate with each other are brought together with a view to recreating, by their juxtaposition, a common denominator catering to the audience's taste.

Preserving indigenous cultures from deculturation is an impossible challenge, short of resorting to a "soft" version of the Indian reservation, as can be found in the Amazon or in the Andaman Islands.[23] Immigration always brings about a cultural reconfiguration, rather than a transferral of original cultures, reconstructing identities around a smaller set of markers, most of which are religious in nature. As I showed in *Holy Ignorance*,[24] deculturation releases religious markers from their cultural framework and gives them a visibility that in turn lends visibility to the decultured faith community. But what is happening today is less a desire to preserve a continuity than to redefine cultural boundaries that delimit identities rather than actual societies.[25] The markers of these reconstructed identities make up a sort of cluster of differences, in total disregard for a hypothetical high culture of origin. The marker can be linguistic, for instance: Gaelic is no longer spoken in Ireland, but the country will use Gaelic "visuals" to exhibit its specificity (institutions and documents sport Gaelic titles or subtitles, without that corresponding to a linguistic practice). The sign can be religious: the Muslim headscarf is now presented in the West, as much by its detractors as by many of its proponents, as the typical marker of "Muslim" identity, regardless of the actual practice of the people wearing it. Rather than define a community of faith, it serves to define an ethnic group recomposed and identified as "Muslims." What is interesting to note is that these markers are never taken from the original high culture (great Arabic poetry does not confer visibility), but always from autonomous anthropological segments: wearing of the headscarf, ways of drinking or eating, and so on. Clifford shows how attempts to recreate an "indigenous culture" in order to revitalise dominated societies produce "self-stereotypes":

> Indigeneity is sustained through media-disseminated images, including a shared symbolic repertoire ("the sacred", "Mother Earth", "shamanism", "sovereignty", the wisdom of "elders", stewardship of "the land"). The images can lapse into self-stereotyping. And they express a transformative renewal of attachments to culture and place. It is difficult to know, sometimes even for participants, how much of the performance of identity reflects deep belief, how much a tactical presentation of self.[26]

The question then arises as to the status of these floating segments. Their loose anchoring in a broader anthropological culture leaves them open to being hijacked and borrowed. Consequently, any use of them arouses suspicions of cultural appropriation. Each community wants to claim its copyright on these floating markers, but they are all the easier to appropriate as they are fashioned, so to speak, as autonomous objects.

But what is cultural re-appropriation if not the ambition to reconstruct a sartorial, culinary or musical folklore? What is authenticity? Once globalisation has occurred, it is impossible to re-appropriate past culture other than by a voluntary act and an appeal to norms, or by winning legal recognition for a cultural practice or object removed from any real culture. Culturalism blossoms on deculturation, but like the cut flowers placed on graves.

Cultural repertoires

Consequently, references to culture are no longer based on an inclusive vision drawing on shared implicit representations, but on repertoires of cultural features, autonomous markers, objects cut off from their conditions of production, in short outside of any social relationship other than the subculture that takes them as its totem. These repertoires come together in a wide variety of contexts that have nothing in common other than being repertoires. I have briefly touched on some of them, such as cuisine. But more importantly I would like to show that a repertoire can relate to very different, even opposing, intentions and actors. I will follow with a few examples.

One is what I would call UNESCO culture. Since it was founded in 1945, the United Nations Educational, Scientific and Cultural Organization has conducted two different policies. The first is the promotion of non-Western high culture; the second, which came later, is the recognition and preservation of anthropological traits raised to the status of cultural objects worthy of a place in the new imaginary museum of world high culture. The first approach thus amounts to "provincialising" Western high culture by demonstrating that it does not have a monopoly on literary genres, or philosophy, or even the human sciences. Ibn Khaldun has been rehabilitated as the founder of sociology; at the same time, the Nobel prize jury for literature rewards great authors from the Third World or minorities (Wole Soyinka in 1986, Naguib Mahfouz in 1988) and major museums such as the MoMA in New York have rehung their collections so that art history no longer appears as Western history. This expansion broadens the space of high culture, but its nature and structure remain intact (great authors produce great works).

The second current of UNESCO's policies tends in the opposite direction: it involves defining humanity's common heritage by selecting objects and practices that mainly come under anthropological culture, crafts and even folklore. The dominance of Western high culture is contested less through the rehabilitation of high cultures from elsewhere than through the levelling of the very notion of high culture in favour of disparate anthropological markers.

The practices selected must be "directly or vicariously linked with events or life traditions, with ideas or religious creeds, with artistic and literary works of exceptional universal significance." Thus on UNESCO's list of "Intangible Cultural Heritage" we find the "art of Neapolitan pizzaiuolo" not far from "Oshi Palav, a traditional meal and its social and cultural contexts in Tajikistan," next to "beer culture in Belgium" (my three favourites), then the "art of Xòe dance of the Tai people of Viet Nam," "Corso culture, flower and fruit parades in the Netherlands," "Pottery-related values, knowledge, lore and practices of the Awajún people," "Compagnonnage, network for on-the-job transmission of knowledge and identities (France)," "Building and use of expanded dugout boats in the Soomaa region," "Camel racing, a social practice and a festive heritage associated with camels (United Arab Emirates and Oman)," "Knowledge, know-how and practices pertaining to the production and consumption of couscous (Algeria, Mauritania, Morocco, Tunisia)," "The Radif of Iranian music," "Holy Week processions in Mendrisio (Switzerland)," "The safeguarding strategy of traditional crafts for peace building (Colombia)," "Shrimp fishing on horseback in Oostduinkerke (Belgium)"—doublecheck position of the shrimp!—"Performance of the Armenian epic of 'Daredevils of Sassoun'," "Alpinism (France, Italy, Switzerland)," logically followed by "Avalanche risk management (Switzerland, Austria)"— though, oddly enough, Italy and France are excluded from the risk prevention culture.[27]

This is not merely a list of miscellanea. It has a strong internal coherence. It is the perfect illustration of the sequencing of cultures into autonomous practices and objects, which I will call, for lack of a better term, "folkloremes," destined to circulate in a global space, and which are therefore homogenised, calibrated and sanitised because they are stripped of anything connoting class conflict, gender or identity. The list equalises a set of practices: those related to high culture (the Iranian Radif or the Armenian epic, for instance), craftsmanship (*compagnonnage*), sociology, religion and folklore. While they are presented as illustrations of national or regional cultures, none of them refer to these cultures as societies, in other words as "total social facts". World culture is an inventory of sequences, often associated with a moral judgment of good practice (peace-building in Colombia). As one might expect, the list sparked furious controversies, making some selections impossible: in October 2008, Fadi Abboud, the president of the Association of Lebanese Industrialists, wanted to sue the state of Israel for appropriating Lebanese culinary culture by exporting hummus and tabbouleh as Israeli foods, whereas he claimed they were traditional Lebanese dishes.[28]

If this type of sequencing works, and triggers such intense reactions (such as the erstwhile controversy over the expansion of McDonald's franchises and today's debate about the spread of kebab shops in European town centres), it is because culture is perceived as a collection of floating markers and not as a total social fact. It is with this conception of culture that people argue about pork or no pork, headscarf or no headscarf, meat or vegan, and other conflicts over school cafeteria menus and dress codes. Markers are of course subject to interpretation, they are perceived as the symbol of something else (the headscarf = the subjugation of women, separatism, etc.), but in very narrow terms: they often operate like pictograms, having an immediate and restricted meaning.

Copyright and folkloremes

Since these elements are floating, they can be hijacked, reused and inserted into new sequences. Attempts to copyright segments of culture and turn them into collections of "folkloremes" is understandable. Each sign is clearly identified and attributed to a given culture. It is less understandable why people today are wrangling over cultural appropriation, which is about far more than plagiarism. Plagiarism always pits two authors who have produced works (the author and the plagiarist) against one another, whereas cultural appropriation is a confrontation between two groups. These groups are usually defined solely by their "ownership" of said folkloremes, as decided by self-proclaimed representatives of the group. This begs the recurrent question: "Who is speaking in whose name?" This phenomenon can be viewed as the performative effect of advocacy, but it is also the sign of the loss of an encompassing culture that can only be reconstructed through fantasy and determination in a living museum.

"Folkloremes" thus circulate easily, and this circulation is what some find unbearable, probably because it is the best marker of the crisis in the notion of culture. Here again, it is norms, in this case copyright norms, that define a culture as a registered trademark and not as the soul of a people or a group. Once a bit of culture is copyrighted, it is taken out of its social (and truly cultural) context, making it the trinket that stands in for an absence.

But it is a one-way struggle: "dominated" cultures protest against their being sequenced and hijacked by the dominant culture.[29] The famous British chef, Jamie Oliver, has been accused of cultural appropriation for launching his brand of "jerk rice": Labour MP Dawn Butler (child of Jamaican immigrants) lambasted the name, wondering whether Oliver even understood the Jamaican style of cooking.[30] The list of "cultural appropriations" looks a lot like the UNESCO inventory of intangible heritage: "818," a brand of tequila created by Kendall Jenner, a member of the Kardashian family with no ties to Mexico; singer Adele's Bantu knots; or the inclusion of a Sikh turban in a 2018 Gucci fashion show (available for purchase at over 700 euros). The critique of cultural appropriation collides with fusion culture: a recent recipe on the Half Baked Harvest website was initially called "Weeknight Ginger Chicken Pho Ga (Vietnamese Chicken Soup)" but had to be renamed "Easy Sesame Chicken and Noodles in Spicy Broth," due to reader pressure, because it presented a fusion version of *pho* that "failed to acknowledge actual elements of pho, including key ingredients, the effort and time required to make it, or even the traditional presentation of the dish."[31] This last criticism is interesting in that it considers the cook's time and labour.

Accusations of cultural appropriation are in fact grounded in a moral judgment: the plight of the dominated is disregarded, and the product of their labour, often exploited, has been stolen. Even if the theory of cultural appropriation refers to the plundering of dominated cultures by conscious or unconscious agents of the dominant culture, it refers the accusers back to the culture that is supposedly their own, thereby denying the universal aspect of the notion of culture. The logic behind this form of taxonomy is that people are only entitled to speak about their own culture, in other words about themselves.

But it is interesting to note that many champions of Western high culture go so far as to deny the very foundation of its claim to dominance, in other words its universality. From Huntington to Renaud Camus and Pascal Bruckner, they view Western culture as a distinct culture, particular to a specific population, that is committing suicide by claiming to understand and integrate other cultures.

For many of these "white" conservatives, the universal nature of their own culture is ultimately a progressive illusion. Renaud Camus asserts that there is something irreducible about French culture that makes it difficult to share when he writes in the same essay:

> Honestly, Jewish journalists on France Culture [radio show] *Panorama* are pushing it too far: first, there are about four out of every five of them in every broadcast, or four out of six, or five out of seven, which on a national and almost official radio station is a clear overrepresentation of a given ethnic or religious group,

then, a few lines down, he claims to speak "in the name of that old native French culture and civilisation to which I belong... and that I regret scarcely hearing anymore, in the very country that was once their own."[32] For if one cannot appropriate the Jamaican cook's jerk, can the Jamaican cook appropriate beef bourguignon or stroganoff? Renaud Camus' remark is not innocuous, because it undergirds his theory of the "great replacement," which has been widely disseminated recently: if replacement were to occur, it would not only be through change in the genetic heritage of a people, but more still through a change of culture, because the existing culture is incapable of assimilating that of a new population.

In other words, the conservative defence of French, European, Western or "white" identity amounts to giving up the claim to universality. Conservatives then strive to make up their own list of patrimonial sequences, artworks, events, monuments and tastes that are allegedly specific to the civilisation they are defending against barbarians, foreigners and cosmopolitans: pork sausage and red wine versus halal couscous, steak cooked rare versus hipster quinoa, folklore and nativity scenes in town halls governed by the right, signage in towns and on streets in a local language that no one speaks anymore (Provençal in Aix-en-Provence). All this is in keeping with a culturalist, and basically pessimistic, vision of what culture and heritage are: the dead hold the living in their grasp, as the saying goes. The living can only bring back and perpetuate what is dead. The debate about culture is infused with alarm and dread on both sides. The nostalgic and the dominated both suffer, exhibiting and demanding reparations for their suffering.

It is interesting to note changes in the vocabulary of appropriation: in the nineteenth century, one spoke of "the soul" of a people or a community; today one speaks of roots, whether those of dominated peoples (Alex Haley's 1976 novel *Roots* and the television adaptation in 1977 marked the start of the quest for African-American identity in the United States, which was no longer confined to the paradigm of "Blacks" and even less of "Negros") or dominant cultures (it was at about the same time, in the 1980s, that people started talking about Europe's "Christian roots"). Conservatives then brought out their collection of patriotic emblems, from Charles Martel to Lyautey and Joan of Arc (images that were often engraved in the nineteenth century by the nationalist left). These emblems have been used as props, for instance in France in the re-enactments staged at Puy-du-Fou theme park, and they turn up regularly in populist projects for rewriting history textbooks and the "national narrative."

Also during the 1980s, in Europe, but leaning more to the left, the historian Pierre Nora developed the idea of "realms of memory:"[33] sequences taken out of the historical continuum that are supposedly meaningful and define who "we" are (as a nation), but which also say what is "good," or embody "what is right" (the Dreyfus affair, Resistance, etc.). We search the past to give meaning to the present in an axiological perspective, in other words through an affirmation of values, a definition of good and bad, from absolute evil (the Holocaust) to controversial issues such as colonisation. The approach in this case is neither anthropological nor historical but deeply moral, because the choice of events and places to commemorate is made according to a narrative, a story of origins, especially concerning the nation. There is hence a very strong link between the selection of markers and value judgements. "Cancel culture" is merely a subset of this axiological reconstruction of the past: it involves depriving "bad" events of commemoration, not erasing them from memory. And here again is the "present-oriented" tendency of contemporary culture: we are living in an eternal present, and at any moment History might make a comeback to alter the present, as in *Terminator*, returning to the past in order to change the present.

The platitude of "ways of life"

The European Union has been built through a series of institutional and political procedures, but never around a shared culture experienced together. Of course, the EU finances a vast array of cultural activities and institutions; of course, it delegates management of national cultural affairs, in accordance with the good old principle of subsidiarity. But it has always stumbled over the question of "the soul" of Europe, in other words culture as a necessity. When the European Commission hears the word culture, it plays *Ode to Joy*, and then moves on.

The process of European construction has always been accompanied by a discourse on European values as liberal values (democracy, human rights, rule of law), but the issue of European culture only arose in 2000, when a debate erupted regarding the mention of Europe's "Christian roots" in the draft for a European constitution.[34] The reference was eventually abandoned; it would not have solved the problem of how to define common European values when there is no consensus on what a common culture might be. Since the 1960s, as discussed previously, the principal liberal values (sexual freedom, feminism, LGBT rights, etc.) have replaced secularised Christian values (natural law, family, gender complementarity). The Catholic Church, through the voice of its supreme pontiffs, denounced the pagan "culture of death" (to quote Benedict XVI, referring to abortion and contraception) supposedly dominant in Europe today; the Catholic Church is still uptight about a Christian identity that is on the wane, but it has proven more open (at least with Pope Francis) to the reception of migrants than the populists who claim the same identity. The reference to "Christian roots" therefore remains merely a mantra, because those advocating a return to actual Christian values and norms in Europe are very much in the minority (except in Poland) and have little influence on politics, even if they lobby actively.[35] Adopting a viewpoint opposite to that of the Catholic Church, the majority of European populists can live with liberal values regarding sexuality, but want to close borders to migrants. In politics, populists are not liberals; they would even like to curb democracy and human rights and therefore dispute the primacy of the rule of law. They challenge the values that justified the construction of Europe, favouring identity over values, and are, in practice, against Islam and immigration. Between liberal values, religious norms and identity in the populist vein, how is it possible to conceive of a European culture?

In the absence of a consensus on what European culture and values might be, in 2019, the Commission therefore decided to appoint a commissioner in charge of "promoting our European way of life." The job description showed clearly that the main mission was to handle immigration, through a mixture of integration and rejection: immigrants should adopt or at least respect the "European way of life."[36] But the identity supposedly being upheld is purely reactive: the issue is how to define immigrants' foreignness and the respects in which Islam is compatible with Europe. Optimists, who identify conditions of compatibility, and pessimists, who see only incompatibility, both define their identity in opposition to something. For the reasons discussed in previous chapters, high culture is never envisioned as a relevant reference and the sociological coherence of European societies is crumbling. In attempting to identify a possible foundation of European culture, we adopt a pseudo-anthropological and very shallow approach, drawing on the smallest common denominators of everyday life.

For how else can this "European way of life" be characterised? At first glance, the phrase appears as a consensual euphemism to designate a European culture that one is reluctant to define further. But it borders on antiphrasis: promoting "ways of life" amounts de facto to admitting the absence of a common culture, not only because there is no consensus about values, but because the very notion of culture no longer has meaning in political and economic liberalism, which is fundamental to the political construction of the European Union. In the job description for the new "way of life" commissioner, the word culture is only mentioned in passing, on a par with sport, of all things (point 1 on the list of objectives: "harness the full potential of culture and sport..., making full use of the European Solidarity Corps and

DiscoverEU programmes"). Meanwhile the "knowledge" to be promoted is defined in the terms of neoliberal excellence, that is, with no relationship to the notion of culture (point 7: "focus on making education more accessible and inclusive, on lifelong learning and on cross-border learning)."[37]

As Wendy Brown notes in the context of the United States, the concept of "way of life" has no positive content and is the bottom rung of culture:

> Put the other way around, if not only rule but subject constitution by culture and religion are equated with organicist orders, then this rule and this constitution are imagined to disappear with the emergence of the autonomous individual; indeed, their vanquishing is the very meaning of such autonomy. For liberal subjects, culture becomes food, dress, music, lifestyle, and contingent values. Culture as power and especially as rule is replaced by culture as mere way of life.[38]

This bottom rung of cultural reference is not a sign of decadence but a consequence of the liberal outlook on society, as Mahmood Mamdani also shows.[39] In his view, political liberalism, as it developed starting in the eighteenth century, places itself above culture and above religion. It defines a political system that has no need for transcendency and can also be applied universally. The rule of law is based on the social compact in the "silence of passions," to quote Rousseau, in which only individual will comes into play. Culture, like religion, can in this regard only interfere with the free interplay of individual wills. That is why "liberals" view culture, particularly in its original form, which is religion (according to Huntington's definition), as an obstacle to "good governance." This is where conservatives (who believe that values are tied to a particular culture) part ways with neoliberals (who believe in the universality of values), whereas politically they were both in the camp that brought Reagan and Thatcher to power in the 1980s. It is therefore logical that political liberalism does not defend

"Europe's Christian roots," even if historians of ideas may point out that certain liberal concepts, such as one's heart of hearts or innermost being, originated in Christianity. Brown sums up well the relationship between political liberalism and culture:

> There is, first, liberalism's conceit about the universality of its basic principles: secularism, the rule of law, equal rights, moral autonomy, individual liberty. If these principles are universal, then they are not matters of culture, which is identified today with the particular, local, and provincial. There is, second, liberalism's unit of analysis, the individual, and its primary project, maximizing individual freedom, which together stand antithetically to culture's provision of the coherence and continuity of groups—an antithesis that positions liberal principles and culture as mutual antagonists. This leads to the third basis on which liberalism represents itself as cultureless: namely, that liberalism presumes to master culture by privatizing and individualizing it, just as it privatizes and individualizes religion. It is a basic premise of liberal secularism and liberal universalism that neither culture nor religion are permitted to govern publicly; both are tolerated on the condition that they are privately and individually enjoyed.[40]

Deculturation is thus part and parcel of the liberal project, which considers that "holistic" societies in which culture supposedly conditions political choices cannot build a good state; they can only be "failed states" or dictatorships. All that remains for Europe, then, is a list of supposedly shared values (feminism, freedom, democracy) that are not in fact truly shared, and a way of life that supposedly characterises average individual behaviour, in other words reflecting statistical conformism. This generally gives rise to a string of platitudes interspersed with incongruities. A good example is the "Starter Kit" for families migrating to the Belgian region of Flanders, put out by the regional government to encourage immigrants to adopt the Flemish way of life, defined in a series of short sentences: "Flemish people like peace and quiet. No noise is permitted after 10 pm. [...]. A traditional Flemish family consists of a father, a mother and children [...]. The Flemish eat chicken, fish, beef and pork. Some people are vegetarians. The Flemish also eat fruit and vegetables, potatoes, pasta and rice."[41]

A way of life: the bottom rung of culture. Utter platitude.

5

COMMUNICATION

A MATTER OF CODES

We can recognise deculturation by the way in which it rules out a shared sense of the self-evident—the implicit meanings we give to actions and words. Coding can be a tool of deculturation precisely because it involves the construction of new relationships based on explicit, unequivocal communication (no innuendo, no double meanings, no allusions). As globalisation tends to "cancel" cultures (or to "provincialise" them), it creates a system of explicit communication that is normative by definition, since any deviation from it would render its meaning unclear, and because it assumes the development of a scale of values outside of any cultural reference and imposed by its self-evident self-proclamation. This coding is more than just a means of communication; it also has to homogenise everything circulating in that space, including culinary and artistic tastes, emotions and bodies.

How are we to understand communication without cultural reference? Of course, this question has not escaped anthropologists. In 1959 Edward Hall differentiated between "high context culture" and "low context culture", defining American culture as "low context" and Japanese culture as archetypally "high context".

> High-context cultures are characterized by a less linear, less direct style of communication, where the listener is expected to be able to judge the intent of the speaker by the context of what is spoken, including body language, facial expressions and tone of voice more than by the actual words spoken. In contrast, low-context cultures communicate in a very linear and direct fashion, with explicit detail.[1]

For me, what is defined here as a difference between two cultures is in fact a breakdown in culture as a whole; for if Hall's theory is true, Japanese culture should resist globalisation, in which it in fact plays a key role. The mistake here is to see cultures as fixed in the representation we have of them at a particular moment in their history (the present for America, a not-so-distant past for Japan).

"Globish" v. English

In designing globalised communication, the first requirement is to identify all the possible "characters" that might feature on a computer keyboard, since it is on this that the universal writing system now depends. In days gone by, typewriters were restricted to alphabets that essentially use letters of the Latin (or Greek and Cyrillic) alphabet. Today any character can be included, including pictograms, Chinese characters and symbols of every kind. The list of possible characters is theoretically infinite and thus open to endless modification; but by convention, only one is accredited, to which everyone can then refer. This is the Unicode Standard, which draws on the Latin, Greek, Cyrillic, Coptic, Sanskrit and other alphabets, invents new possible letters, and includes punctuation marks, symbols (such as $ and £), special characters (#, &) and so on. This is the physical medium of universal communication.

COMMUNICATION

However, it is not (or not yet) possible to sidestep the use of a real language. Every attempt to invent a universal language (such as Esperanto) has failed. Meanwhile, languages that are simply communicative (such as the *lingua franca* used in Mediterranean ports from the fifteenth century and other pidgins) have never become official or acquired a written form. Their status remains provisional, occasional, confined to social categories (languages used in ports, by traders or between slaves and their masters). When they do come to replace mother-tongues—and are then "creoles"—they become "natural" languages linked to particular societies and cultures, thereby losing their role in supra-cultural communication. But what has become interesting in recent decades is the spontaneous worldwide process by which a real language (English) has been decultured and simplified to turn it into a universal language of communication that can function stably in any cultural context and without replacing natural languages. Unlike pidgins and creoles, this language is carried by elites and is known as "Globish".[2]

This language initially requires a limited number of words (around 1500, plus a few dozen belonging to technical vocabularies). It is true that individual speakers may have a far greater lexical range but, since they do not know the extent of their interlocutor's knowledge, to be sure of being understood they will spontaneously reduce their vocabulary, choosing those words that seem most likely to be familiar to both—for example saying "brothers and sisters" rather than "siblings". In the same way, literary allusions are to be avoided (with exceptions such as "to be or not to be", the quotation from *Hamlet* that has become a collusional tic). This leads to a paradox whereby speakers whose mother tongue and culture are English become hard to understand (because they use too many words and make too many spontaneous allusions to cultural references) and also find it hard to understand when spoken to in Globish. For Globish is a language constructed solely through the practice of communication and not through any previous effort to simplify English. Consequently, true English speakers are less likely to realise that the process occurs in a world where they are in the minority.[3] The European University Institute, where I work, is a very good example: almost all of the administration and all the courses are undertaken in English, but with very few mother-tongue English speakers and in interactions where speakers of French, Italian, Hungarian, Dutch, German, Spanish and others must be able to understand each other without the assistance of an English speaker. Consequently, consensus develops on what should be said in Globish, without reference to the usual forms validated by English (one example picked at random: we have "sickness insurance", as in French, German and Dutch, rather than the "health insurance" of English-speaking countries). The European Union is a marvellous laboratory of Globish, even more so since Brexit. It develops the language without reference either to its original speakers or to any specific culture. So the aim is not to acculturate Globish, to link it to a new culture (other than metaphorically), but to preserve its position outside of any culture.

Eurospeak, the written language used by the European Commission, is the bureaucratic variant of Globish. Without going into detail, we need only consider the instructions that the Commission gives for translations: "Expressions which are too specific to one language should therefore be avoided as far as possible" (Guideline 5.3.1).[4] Avoiding anything specific to one language is a good way to sum up the aim of Globish: to eradicate cultural reference.

Therefore, it is not that English is becoming dominant, along with its cultural underpinning, but that the use of English is becoming decultured. This is why the linguistic phenomenon definitely does not reflect an Americanisation of world culture. The aim is to avoid any misunderstanding and any need to refer to implicit understandings that might not necessarily be shared. Jokes are banned and emotions have to be expressed explicitly using an emoji with a pre-defined meaning. Emotion is allowed, of course, but it must be immediately understood by addressees, wherever they may come from, so it is "sourced" from a list that, while remaining open, is pre-prepared.

The same phenomenon affects body language, which as we know has deep cultural roots and is the source of many misunderstandings. In the Middle East, for example, moving your chin upwards while clicking your tongue means "no", whereas in the West moving your head up and down means "yes", while a smile is not a universal indication of benevolence and friendship. These are the stuff of entertaining travel stories. But in global communication there is a tendency to suppress body language or to confine it to predetermined gestures with clear meanings (such as the "high five", when two speakers slap their right hands together with fingers spread to congratulate each other; hugging, when one person puts their arms around another as a sign of sympathy; or joining one's two hands to say thank you). The best approach is to limit physical contact in communication. This limitation is already under way, as noted by an American specialist in management training:

> Because members of global, intercultural and geographically-dispersed teams and work groups often communicate primarily by electronic mail, telephone or text chat, body language and other nonverbal behaviors are often indistinguishable in conversations, leaving the parties with nothing but the written or spoken word.[5]

The pandemic and the expansion of distance working linked to mask-wearing have merely accelerated a trend that is rooted in the logic of globalisation itself. The paradox is that, while we read less and less in lockdown, we texted more and more. Because this form of writing transcribes speech, it is not "literature". It is "disembodied", sound-proofed, sanitised, toned down, and its syntax remains that of oral language. This written speech is located beyond the classic contrast of "oral" and "written" language. It is speech that does not require the other speaker to be physically present.[6] It has neither the depth of written language nor everything that emanates from a physical presence. It flattens a conversation to the point where people often settle for ready-made phrases and suggestions offered by predictive text.

Clearly this deculturation disturbs that cornerstone of relations between language and culture that is translation. How can we translate without reference to culture—or rather, when we neutralise culture? Machine translation is a good example of this flattening of knowledge. It works reasonably well (at any rate from English to other major languages), which suggests that it will get better and better. But its mode of working is not that of classic translation, which seeks the meaning beyond the words: "The machine does not translate, it calculates the statistical estimate of the best translation of these two (three, four, etc.) words by comparing them to all the other translations in its memory".[7]

The autistic spectrum

I would compare this new relationship to communication with a curious phenomenon that seems to go with it. This is the expansion of the domain of autism.[8] More precisely, it is the expansion of interest in autism, which in the last few years has morphed from a terrible psychiatric illness into a trend. This trend had perhaps already started at the time of the release of the film *Rain Man* (directed by Barry Levinson, 1988), or even at the time of the famous Mr Spock in *Star Trek*, the 1960s TV series (when Dr McCoy described Spock as an "unfeeling automaton" and the "most cold-blooded man [he had] ever known", Spock replies, "Why, thank you, Doctor").[9] Today we read accounts of "coming out": "how I discovered I was on the autistic spectrum".[10] For we now speak of the "autistic spectrum", the illness having been reclassified in its benign forms as behaviour that is slightly peculiar, which others may indeed find disconcerting, but which is ultimately perfectly adapted to the new forms of coding.

The "autistic spectrum" that once seemed to shut an individual away in depressing solipsism (see Bruno Bettelheim's book *The Empty Fortress*) now becomes the quintessential syndrome of the new conditions of communication. As Élaine Hardiman-Taveau explains,

> Autistic people with Asperger's are unable to translate anything that is implicit or abstract. Implicit elements dictate how we behave with another person—according to their sex, age, accent and so on [...] Although we are not aware of it, there is a small package that directs our behaviour in relation to the other person [...] However, in the domains of their own skills, which are specific to each individual, they may be "better than the rest". This is a value that few employers are able to discern behind the social difficulties.[11]

Some typical traits of autism (not understanding implicit meanings, concern for the precision of terms and the correspondence between word and thing) now seem to make autistic people better able to master the dominant techniques of communication. In fact there is an entire Wikipedia page discussing the contributions of collaborators on the autistic spectrum and advising the non-autistic on how to approach them: "Avoid ambiguity wherever you possibly can. People on the Autism spectrum can have very literal minds [...] Be *very clear*; avoid phrases like 'You should do...' and use words like 'do', 'don't', 'never', 'always' instead."[12] This is precisely what is required by coding in general. Socialisation is secondary and any polysemy, irony or nuance is a source of error; the autistic mode "does the job".

Of course, I have no problem with facilitating the integration of autistic people into the world of work; I simply note that this desire to promote them on the market is neither an act of charity nor (or not solely) the manifestation of a cynical intent to make money from disabilities. Instead it is a way of recognising that the new forms of communication and coding are congruent with those characteristics that once gave autistic people their strangeness: their fear of all that is implicit; their need for systematic explanations; their indifference to the cultural nature of social codes; and their desire for norms, the absence of which they regard, not as a source of freedom but, on the contrary, of anxiety when faced with the profound obscurity of interpersonal relationships. On the autistic spectrum everything turns out to be code, and what had been a problem of socialisation becomes an advantage in the new culture.

This does not mean that the autistic spectrum has no place for emotion—quite the reverse, since those who are on the spectrum say that they are overwhelmed by emotion and seek to protect themselves from it. So the next challenge, which is to establish unequivocal communication detached from all culture, involves coding emotions as well, rather than repressing them.

Coding emotions: emojis and emoticons

The role of emojis and emoticons is to represent an emotion or feeling through an assemblage of typographical marks (emoticons) or pictograms (emojis). The pictograms are chosen from an open list, usually in Unicode. New examples can be invented and there are observable cultural variations in their use. For while everyone draws from the same set, there are local variations in the frequency with which a particular type is used. It would be a mistake to regard emojis purely as replicas of gestures or immediately recognisable facial expressions, for these are already culturally coded. Neurologists have sought to establish a semantics of facial expressions, regardless of culture, by classifying emotions according to the movement of the facial muscles. The result is the Facial Action Coding System (FACS). But emojis are not based on this, and do not reflect a physiologically authentic emotion which could thus claim an anthropometric universality that pre-exists cultures.[13] They have their own logic, establishing an arbitrary link between a drawing and an emotion, without reference to a particular culture.

To enable the system to work anywhere in the world, all that is required is for everyone to accept the idea of a global classification of emotions as discrete elements, in other words as a finite number of precisely differentiated elements, as long as more can be added. But in no case can there be any grey areas, for neither nuance nor individual variation are allowed. Complex emotions (laughter mixed with tears, Schadenfreude) remain juxtapositions of discrete elements.[14] Emojis offer a finite set of ready-to-cry, ready-to-laugh emotions.

This codification may seem artificial or reductive—and so it is! But fundamentally, while it goes without saying that emotions are always expressed in a cultural context (modesty, honour, shame and love are never raw emotions) and, to a degree, already coded by a culture, does this mean that they cannot be constructed and coded outside of that culture? Culturally constructed emotions overflow the meaning they are given. They need a background and they refer to a shared imaginary. Literature constructs this imaginary by commenting on and staging emotion (the oft-discussed cathartic effect of theatre), whereas emotion expressed in emojis has no need for comment. It is possible—and this has been tested—to imagine a book entirely in emojis. But is it then still literature, or is it a simple example of communication, a linear narrative? It is the status of literature itself that is in question here.

In reality, the coding of emotions is not a new thing; it is the process of de-contextualisation and recomposition that is new.

So there is nothing to stop a robot having feelings; they would just need to be "coded".[15] What is new is that this system of coding tends to deny (or deprive of pertinence) the subjective depth that underpins emotion. Everyone can recognise themselves in the code because the emotion is firstly a stereotype and secondly a marketing teaser.[16] "Ready-to-cry" is as available as "ready-to-wear", accessible to all.

Why Japan?

The Japanese origin of emojis begs some questions: how can emojis be at once outside culture and products of a particular culture? If Japanese culture is high-context, how did it come to produce the most effective tools of semantic globalisation, in other words signifiers detached from all culture, as is also true of manga?

The argument that manga and emojis are part of a profoundly Japanese cultural context is doubtless true, but it does not explain their globalisation.[17] My hypothesis is that they became globalised because they now refer to a Japan that is fictional, and which serves to produce sets of globalisable signs, no doubt because the challenge of globalisation is greater in Japan than elsewhere. Japanese culture—including manga, which is so deeply rooted within it—has adopted a "deculturation software", the aim being to deculture the products of its own society so that they can circulate throughout the world. This is why it is as wrong to speak of the Japanisation of the world as of its Americanisation. What works is not the universality of Japanese culture, but its capacity to produce objects that "look Japanese", that have the aura of the original brand—which is reputed to be incommunicable—while denying its incommunicability. If Japanese culture has become an element in globalisation, it is because no culture remains opaque or indifferent to it. In other words, the cultural depth of the country is merely a historical ruse in order to sell its authenticity as an agent of general deculturation. In *The Empire of Signs*, Roland Barthes gives a very subtle analysis of how it is possible to settle into the world of signs (and enjoy it) without concern for the culture from which they emerged. Elena Giannoulis observes that "Japan in the emojiverse is analogous to Tokyo in Barthes's fictive Japan".[18]

So there is nothing behind the emoji (or rather what is behind it is not regarded as pertinent and does not matter). It gives literal expression to an emotion that is flat, in other words not open to interpretation, unambiguous, instantly comprehensible by any other person. As such, is it still an emotion? No, it is simply an emoji that refers only to itself.

But now that this requirement for the unambiguity of the sign has been established, we are witnessing an evolution in the opposite direction among specialists of emoji communication, as the creation of emojis endlessly expands to enable individuals to express themselves to best effect according to their particular culture and sensibility, in what looks like a negation of the very reason for the existence of these signs. It seems that users are refusing to take the system's logic to its extreme and are trying to "save" the concept of culture.[19]

In other words, culture seems to be making a comeback. But is this really the revenge of anthropological culture? What is coming back under the name of culture (a set of interpretative variations that blur the emoji's main function of providing unequivocal meaning) does not seem to be a pre-existing form. In reality, the variations of emojis are subcultural practices (particularly of youth culture) rather than those of national cultures. Giannoulis makes this point:

> even supposedly "fixed meanings" can suffer from individual inter-
> pretations. Hence, the creative use of emoji and of emoji combina-
> tions resembles a language that the respective community is con-

stantly transforming by simply using it. We experience special shifts in meaning, for example, in the language of youth, which often puzzles adults.[20]

The fact that the code turns or extends into language is no surprise, but it is not enough to recreate a "culture". On the contrary, it shows how floating modes of communication can become established and renew themselves, without acquiring the status of anthropological or high culture.

The hunt for the unsaid: from the unconscious to confession

The coding of communications and cultures clearly has an impact on imaginaries, since these suppose either transcendence, which is above and beyond communication, or an underpinning to communication. It thus affects two domains in particular: religion and psychoanalysis, the beyond and the beneath. In France, moreover, both these domains have fallen victim to a broad offensive in recent years: religion is suspected of hypocrisy, which is not in itself new, but crucially it is accused of concealing something other than the mystery of the elevation of souls (for example, male libido and priestly power, as has been shown by the recent scandals related to paedocriminality); psychoanalysis is accused of being unscientific and even of verging on quackery.

Religion, as I studied it in *Holy Ignorance*, has seen two parallel and connected movements, secularisation and neo-fundamentalism, both of which relate to the religious imaginary. Within Protestantism the mainstream church has largely become secularised, emphasising ethics over mysticism, while the evangelical currents have conversely turned to normativity (against abortion and same-sex marriage). Protestant fundamentalism perfectly follows the line of codes and norms, as can be seen, for example, in its obsession with controlling sexuality through practices such as conversion therapy—where people who are homosexual have to "recode" themselves as heterosexual—the public confession of sins or checking for signs of pregnancy to prevent the possibility of abortion.

On the Catholic side, in the interests of *aggiornamento*, the Second Vatican Council of 1962 sought to render explicit the mysteries of the faith—replacing Latin with the vernacular languages was a demythification (or rather a demystification, removing the aura of incomprehensibility that had a magical aspect). From this point of view, the abandonment of Latin was entirely logical. How can one be explicit in a language one does not understand? But, as I indicated in *Is Europe Christian?*, translation brought with it a secularisation of notions such as hell, the devil and penitence (which was replaced by "reconciliation"). The same concern for rationalisation led to a change in the ritual, with the adoption of more everyday actions: the priest faces the congregation instead of turning his back on them; the eucharist is passed from hand to hand. Conversely, those who called for the ritual to be maintained did so in the name of mystery, magic, the power of the unsaid and emotion that cannot be emoji-ed, criticising Vatican II for "flattening" the religious world in the name of explicitness by bringing it back down to earth.

For both Protestantism and the logic of Vatican II, a return to the "true religion" paradoxically requires the rite to be reduced to its secular state. The movement known as Catholic integralism, which rejects this "updating", is not (unlike evangelical Protestantism) a form of fundamentalism, since it does not claim to return to the pure, literal truth of the text, but rather to what is felt to be an original religious culture (in this case developed in the sixteenth century by the Council of Trent).

One point of tension between the tradition of the Catholic Church and new culture is the practice of confession, or rather the Seal of Confession, the duty of priests to ensure total confidentiality. The revelation of paedocriminal acts committed within the Catholic Church has recently accelerated the questioning of this absolute secrecy, and priests are increasingly being encouraged by the law to denounce penitents who have confessed to paedocriminal behaviour. However, in seeking to obtain the confession of sins, the practice of confession is driven by the intention to make things explicit and contained by two limitations. The first of these is original sin, the one thing that confession cannot absolve. A root of evil remains underground and cannot be redeemed until the light of resurrection dawns. The truth of confession is therefore not unequivocal, it relates to a mystery. Secondly, everything that is made explicit remains sealed by the Seal of Confession. So there is no transparency. The obligatory removal of the seal threatens this private, sacred space, which would then be brought into the light to face the judgment of temporal inspection. In this case, such an outcome might be desirable for moral and judicial reasons. But beyond the issue of paedocriminality (as we can be sure that other causes will also justify breaking the Seal of Confession),[21] it is the very notion of sacrament that is under threat, in other words the vertical ordering of the world, from the Fall to Redemption. Here too we see the flattening of the world in the rejection of both heaven and root.

The critique of psychoanalysis is of a similar order, in the sense that it rejects the mysteries of the unconscious. It began as soon as psychoanalysis became known, but in the twenty-first century it has taken a new turn. By contrast, Freudian thought and its various avatars were an integral part of post-1968 culture in France and regarded as a legitimate form of therapy, for which public health insurance would pick up the tab.

Since *Le Livre noir de la psychanalyse* and many attempts to make psychoanalytic practice prohibited by law (see for example the debate on the Accoyer amendment of 2003 on the regulation of psychotherapy), the attack has been made in the name of science, represented by psychiatry and cognitivist psychology.[22] These disciplines do not work on the unconscious but on behaviours, which they seek to identify and treat. They deal with psychic disturbance by prescribing either medication linked to a nomenclature of disorders or else self-correction using behaviourist techniques (all based on more or less sophisticated forms of behaviourism). These approaches include group therapies, which level the originality of individuals by reducing their behaviours, such as addictions, to generic traits shared by all. So although therapies of the "Alcoholics Anonymous" variety begin with a form of confession, they turn it into a simple technique for self-correction, on a path marked in stages (identifying progress and backsliding) that is common to all and which individuals are supposed to complete through willpower and imitation. This profoundly normative system is based on a calibration of behaviours that is reminiscent of neoliberal benchmarking.

The resurgence of psychiatry to the detriment of psychoanalysis has been accompanied by an expansion in the classification of disorders. If instances of deviant or problematic behaviour are to be reduced to measurable and observable deviations from a "normality" defined as adaptation to society and an absence of "suffering", this requires a proliferation of classifying categories. In the years 1980–94, the number of psychological disorders identified in the DSM or *Diagnostic and Statistical Manual of Mental Disorders*, which the American Psychiatric Association regularly updates, increased from 185 to 350.[23] And this was at a time when some "disorders" ceased to be classified as such, including homosexuality. Each disorder is based on the "objective" observation of symptoms, unrelated to the history of individuals or the cultural context. The sequencing of behaviours recalls the model of DNA sequencing. As there is no boundary between healthy and sick, disorders are defined as spectrums along which a cursor moves. As with autism, the increasing number of psychological disorders is not the result of people being increasingly "mad", but the grouping together of certain behavioural or character traits to define a pathological state. One of the best-known new disorders is Post-Traumatic Stress Disorder (PTSD), which affected millions of veterans of the two world wars, but was only "discovered" after the Vietnam war and now flourishes on every occasion where people have been subject to violent situations.[24] Speaking of disorders rather than illness also makes it possible to establish a continuum, a scale from "well" to deep pathology, in a quantitative continuity with no qualitative leap. As in the village of Dr Knock, everyone is sick, but not everyone knows it. For this scale of disorders is flat: it refers only to itself.

* * *

Real individuals (with their unconscious, their history, their areas of light and shadow and their contradictions) are no longer a point of reference, still less an excuse. They are judged on sequenced words and deeds, taken out of context and objectified on a moral (or ethical) scale.

In all these domains, there is no longer any reference that could endow individuals with any "interiority", be it the unconscious, history or culture.[25] This has come about according to a market model that turns everything into pieces of merchandise defined by comparable criteria (how does it fulfil its function?). Individuals are thus "coded" and integrated into a nomenclature of behaviours. This fascination with behavioural science goes far beyond the split between conservatives and liberals. The evangelical Liberty University has no department of humanities, but a very large "School of Behavioral Sciences."[26]

6

CAN WE CHOOSE OUR SEX OR RACE?

Coding and sequencing go hand in hand with an expansion of taxonomies. We classify and create categories by selecting a few markers that define a person's identity. These markers are no longer adjectives (homosexual, Catholic, fat, black, white, etc.), but have become nouns. In other words, they have ceased to be qualifiers, instead stating the person's substance. We do not ask whether Proust was homosexual or Jewish, but whether he is a homosexual author or a Jewish author. The same goes for women, black people, white people and so on. The next stage is to obtain recognition for that identity, on the grounds of the suffering caused by non-recognition. Sex and race are the two main domains of this new fight, since both raise the problem of nature in its biological form. Does a nature resistant to free coding still exist?

Talking sex

Why is sexuality now caught in a system of normative coding, where the question of explicit consent becomes central? Because sexuality has become autonomous in relation to culture. The revolution of the 1960s freed sexuality from cultural constraint—desire is good, culture is repression. Fifty years later it is obvious that this sexual liberation has not abolished relations of domination while simultaneously making them less tolerable: rape, sexual harassment, femicides, paedocriminality and incest have become more visible as they become less and less socially acceptable. This reaction is not indicative of a desire to go back to a conservative culture centred on the family, but of sexual liberation turning on itself. The #MeToo movement has unfolded in parallel to the expansion of LGBTQI rights, the legalisation of various forms of artificial procreation and the recognition of gender fluidity. As there is no consensus on the new rules of the game, in other words on the limits of freedom, desire and the recomposition of sexual identities, we are faced both with greater violence—or rather greater visibility of a violence that can no longer hide in tacit silences and family secrets—and a demand for codification and normativity. It is now accepted that consent cannot be implicit. So it must be explicitly expressed. But according to what code?

We have gone from "peace and love" to "#MeToo", from the harmony of desires to the denunciation of patriarchal domination and its violence, which is not only symbolic but also physical. Sexual freedom seems to have enabled a new type of male domination that is more brutal because it is no longer culturally contained (by gallantry, for example) and can thus only be countered by the imposition of normative codes of behaviour, backed up by legal constraints.

The autonomisation of the sexual domain in relation to the dominant culture has also led to the development of pornography as a sexual sequence detached from any kind of social relations and from all communication. Pornography is a caricature of the autonomy of sexual relations. It is constructed using a finite set of coded sequences in a module comprising positions, size, time and sounds, always leading to the same result: orgasm, with nothing after it (and almost nothing before). These sequences do not open the way to an imaginary (unlike eroticism). Pornography as the coding of actions and sexual vignettes has always existed (see the graffiti in Pompeii), but it is now freely accessible to all on the internet, and is no longer contained within the margins to which it was formerly consigned by the dominant culture (from toilets to brothels). Of course, I am not claiming that pornography is the contemporary model of sexuality, but that in it we find, as caricature—in other words in almost pure form—the relationship between the autonomy of desire, the coding of relations and domination.

The autonomy of desire, as it was formulated in the sexual liberation that came out of Sixties culture, is understood in terms of both culture and biology. The distinction between desire (construction of an imaginary) and drive (simple physiological need) is fundamental in all the psychoanalysis-influenced literature that accompanied this movement in the second half of the twentieth century. In elevating biological nature, desire goes above and beyond culture (said to seek to control sexual freedom and to fix sexual roles, which is indeed the case). Culture is perceived as constraint, censure and limitation, and not as a space of freedom. It is also understood as a patriarchal system, legitimising male domination. So the discourse of sexual freedom seems at first sight to be a discourse of liberation for men and women alike.

This vision is not new. The utopia of a "primitive", sexually free and thus harmonious society was present throughout the Age of Enlightenment (see Diderot's *Supplément au voyage de Bougainville*). But this idea that sexual liberation is the mother of all liberations never became a reality. It is perhaps no coincidence that the Marquis de Sade, an Enlightenment man, pushed the bounds of sexual freedom in a different direction of absolute desire and thus of domination. Sade's profound modernity may relate to his vision of sex as coding, played to a full house. This is no longer the old tradition of erotic literature in which sexuality is placed within the narrative, aesthetic and cultural frameworks of a particular society (Boccaccio's *Decameron*), but an attempt to autonomise sexual practices in a decontextualised scenario, the prototype of which is *120 Days of Sodom*. There is an obsession with sequencing and explicitness, unfolding in a pre-ordained, normative ritual, where any misdemeanour or deviation from the script is punished. The code must absorb the entire imaginary and the sequence can end only in death—not through sadism (so to speak), but the death of desire itself. What is particularly interesting about this is that Sade was a highly cultured man, and yet the precision of his language precisely helps to eliminate anything cultural from the procedure of desire.

If coding is indeed the consequence of deculturation, which is the thesis of this book, we can see why pornography has become mundane. But the implication of this is that coding is also the only way to contain sexual violence that is no longer structured by culture, in other words that is no longer both channelled and legitimated. Honour killings, crimes of so-called "passion" and some types of rape are typical sexual crimes, but throughout history they have been excused (by "attenuating circumstances" in court), and indeed legitimated, while being also contained by cultures.[1] When the cultural excuse ceases to be acceptable, they appear as pure violence. But what is the motivation for this violence?

Two almost concomitant cases serve as illustrations: the Cologne assaults and the Harvey Weinstein affair. On 31 December 2015 in Cologne, Germany, women were sexually assaulted by several hundred men during the New Year celebrations. The court sentences revealed that the perpetrators included a high proportion of men of Muslim origin.[2] The commentators thus associated the sexual assaults with the men's "Muslim" or "Middle Eastern" culture, depending on whether they wanted to emphasise religion or ethnicity (in both cases, sexual assault was related to a culture, in the anthropological sense of the term).[3] The response was then to impose "European values" of respect for women on immigrants from a different culture. This affair played a role in the appointment of a commissioner for the "European way of life", discussed in Chapter 4.

But the Weinstein affair (involving a powerful American film producer, following a number of complaints from actresses) and the #MeToo movement (launched in 2017 in the wake of this affair), followed in France by "Balance ton porc" [squeal on your pig], led to a reversal of perspective. No one started by criticising Judeo-Christian patriarchy. The problem was no longer the culture of the assailant (reflecting all races and religions, educated, cultivated, and even a great public defender of "Western values"), but his very nature as a male, an animal, a pig. In this case the culture of rape was no longer linked to one anthropological culture, but to a constant (of debatable origin) that runs through every culture and historical period. Yet if it is universal, this constant can only reflect an inherent nature. It might be said that nature has replaced culture as the origin of violence.[4] It is apparently impossible to find egalitarian or truly matriarchal societies (being matrilinear or matrilocal does not necessarily mean the absence of patriarchal power). We can of course follow Brown and Mamdani in noting that Western culture always sees itself as comprised of autonomous individuals,[5] and always attributes others with a cultural holism in which individual behaviours can be explained by cultural constraints alone.[6] But the existence of a prejudice changes nothing with regard to the issues we are considering. On the contrary, the decoupling of culture and sexuality is there before our eyes. The responses to #MeToo in other cultures clearly show that this is not a purely Western issue and that, to put it simply, globalisation is at work. We shall return later to what this means for the universality or otherwise of values.

Western reactions to the Weinstein affair are very interesting. While condemnation of the man was widely shared, a movement emerged, notably in France, that protested against the witch-hunt, the new censorship and the return of puritanism. Opposition to the witch-hunt (or perhaps wizard-hunt in this case) often adopted a "cultural" argument, asserting that the French culture of seduction policed itself through the practice of gallantry. Christine Boutin, at the time leader of the Parti Chrétien de France, the country's only overtly Catholic party, became the apologist for "French ribaldry", followed or preceded by the Causeur website, home of grumpy nostalgia and falling standards (everything in the past was good, so sex-pests were not all bad).[7] In general these were also the groups and sites that constantly denounced sexual assaults committed by Muslims because of their religion.[8] In other words, the rapists are the Others.[9] But, like any discourse of nostalgia, this defence of a French tradition is also an indication of deculturation. Gallantry, seduction and ribaldry have ceased to be viable defences in court, as has the cultural argument in support of female genital mutilation (still usable in the 1990s). The cultural excuse no longer works, either for immigrants or for those "of French stock". Deculturation is the same for everyone.

In this way, the autonomisation of sex in relation to culture brings with it a brutalisation of relations between genders. It is true that gallantry was profoundly inegalitarian, but it was also deeply cultural and based on codes that in themselves expressed a culture, through a vision of the place of each gender, the domestication of raw sexuality, and shared understandings in which each was implicitly supposed to know their role and keep to their place. The crisis of culture automatically means that nature—whether real or fantasised—surfaces in the purely biological form of drives. Rape drugs become a metaphor for the raw sexual act (and hence rape) that is within any man's reach.

When the cultural coding of sexuality disappears, a new and explicit coding must be established.

Social contract, sexual contract

The Enlightenment advanced the theory of the social contract to ground society in the freedom of individual actors; this same concept resurfaced in the 1960s, this time in the form of the sexual contract.[10] The contract is a way of establishing consent, thus ensuring the freedom of each party in sexual relations. Of course the social contract is presented as a fiction: men, "in the silence of passions" (Rousseau), decide to constitute themselves as citizens and to establish a tacit agreement that forms civil society and defines relations with the state. This "silence of passions" then has to be guaranteed in the sexual contract—a tall order by definition.

As Pateman has shown, in its philosophical genealogy the social contract, intended as the foundation of the rule of law by consent, is based on a profound gender disparity. All eighteenth-century theorists of the social contract excluded women from the pact, on the grounds that they were aligned with passion and nature, and thus incapable of leaving the state of nature behind, as the social contract required. This original dissymmetry is also present in the sexual contract, which is supposed to base sexual relations on consent between two equal parties. "The (sexual) contract is the vehicle through which men transform their natural right over women into the security of civil patriarchal right".[11] Pateman goes on to cite Locke, who says that wives must be subject to their husbands, since "generally the Laws of mankind and customs of Nations have ordered it so; and there is, I grant, a Foundation in Nature for it."[12]

This is the basic problem: is male domination rooted in nature, or is it a product of culture? If, as Locke thinks, every society legitimates a very diverse range of patriarchal domination, the only way to establish equality is to leave culture behind, in other words, to move towards deculturation. If on the other hand patriarchal culture is merely a statistical phenomenon (the great majority of cultures are patriarchal, but some allow the emancipation of women), we can understand the quest for equality in terms of good and bad culture. In the 1980s the anthropologist Nicole-Claude Mathieu was a pioneer of the critical analysis of anthropology on women.[13] Her critique coincides with that of Pateman: in anthropology (which generally adopts the discourse used by a society in relation to itself, or more precisely what anthropologists understand of that discourse), men are aligned with culture and women with nature, which was precisely the argument of the philosophers of the social contract.[14]

But if male domination is universal, if it does not depend on any given culture, then it must accord with nature. The rise of neuroscience, sociobiology and ethology that is now apparent in the study of human beings reinserts us into the continuity of our animality. One recurrent characteristic is the use of evolution to explain human sexuality: males seek as many opportunities as possible to pass on their genes (including conquests and rape), while females are primarily interested in finding the best male, who will provide good offspring and defend the home.[15] This analysis ignores one detail: in no societies, including those described as primitive, do we find filiation based solely on male philandering; they all codify the framework of sexual relations fairly rigorously. But I am not going to explore here the scientific validity of analyses of this kind, I simply note that they have been relayed in works of popular science that seek to explain (and thus in a way to justify) human behaviours, including homosexuality.[16] Reading this literature is enough to make your head spin, for in it you learn that polygamy exists in nature (among monkeys) but so does monogamy (pigeons), that the female may be submissive, dominant, or even devour the male (the praying mantis), that she may sacrifice herself for her young, or on the contrary eat her children (rabbits), that the male may share in bringing up the young or pay them no attention at all—in other words, everything is in nature and vice-versa. As ever, the argument from nature leads to no conclusions about culture. We are going around in circles.

What interests me here is not to conceptualise relations between nature and culture, but to look at the way in which nature has resurfaced in contemporary debates. On the one hand, it is present in traditionally conservative perspectives: our societies and sexual identities are rooted in nature, there is a biological continuum, and thus a degree of determinism in our behaviours, which means that they require social training; this is the point of culture, insofar as it opens the way to a transcendence that elevates human beings above animality. But this assertion of continuity between humans and animals has also been taken up on the left, in antispeciesism and the animal rights movement: this time it is animals that must be recognised in their continuity with humans, as subjects under the law. Instead of looking upwards, above animals, we look downwards, below humans. The Enlightenment rejected civic rights for women because they were too close to animals (functioning on instinct) and antispeciesists defend animal rights in the name of the same continuity, considered retrospectively.

Since sexual encounters are less and less determined by any cultural and sociological context (or at least so it seems to their protagonists) and result more from chance or intentional dating, the way they unfold is understood in terms of the paradigm of the sexual contract as a sub-set of the social contract. Sociologists can of course show that these encounters, which seem free of

social constraints, in practice obey other forms of social determinism. But what counts here is the perception of the protagonists. And since this is a contract, the terms are supposed to be
explicit and are thus a matter of "consent". This requires a system
of communication that is perfectly explicit. Once extracted from
a cultural context regarded as alienating, sexuality is recomposed
in coding that is primarily explicit, but which also turns into a
normative system.

Sexual consent and pornographic coding

The central issue is consent. Following an increase in complaints
of sexual harassment and rape from the 2010s, and the new
awareness and readiness to speak out illustrated by the #MeToo
movement, the courts and disciplinary bodies of different institutions, including universities, adopted ever clearer and more precise definitions of the conditions of sexual consent. The movement began in the United States and developed in Europe. It is
neither linear nor always consistent, but over the long term there
has been a trend to require explicit consent. But what is the
object of this consent? Courts have considered not only the
sexual relation itself but also its sequencing, as illustrated by the
charges levelled against Julian Assange, accused of rape by two
women.[17] The issue is not simply to decide whether or not the
complainant initially consented to sexual relations, but whether,
at every stage (undressing, condom use, penetration while
asleep), consent can be established or not. Why is it not enough
to decide whether there was initial consent to the act? As often,
this type of consent is hard to define: she didn't really want to,
but went along with it all the same, on certain conditions—condom use—that he did not respect, but agreed to spend another
night with him anyway, during which he penetrated her while
she was asleep. At this point there are two solutions: either we

accept that sexuality cannot be contractualised, or, conversely, we regard it as a series of specific acts that are describable, in which every sequence can be accepted or refused. This would amount to renouncing the experience of sexuality as an undivided whole, in which dark and light are inextricably linked. Such sequencing is ultimately pornographic, in other words each segment of the sexual act is autonomous with respect to the encounter taken as a whole, and to any emotional relations that may exist between the protagonists. But, unlike pornography, each sequence is conceptualised with a value judgement intended to strip it of any relation of domination. The psychoanalyst and philosopher Clotilde Leguil notes the difficulty of making consent explicit:

> There is no informed consent. This phrase, which relates to the legal and medical domains, masks the fact that there is always an element of darkness and enigma in consent [...]. It is because consent engages the body, and is in fact a bodily experience rather than an act of reason, that it includes obscurity for the individual, which sometimes leads them to let things go further than they wanted.[18]

But in the logic of coding and the rejection of any obscure elements that characterises contemporary deculturation, this position is no longer seen as legitimate, which renders the practice of psychoanalysis, and indeed of philosophy, somewhat hazardous.

Coding then becomes normative. Here we will provide some concrete examples of a general trend, which is undoubtedly more complex and varied than we can convey here, but which seems to me to be summed up by a Californian law. The first article of a law passed in 2014 by the Senate of the State of California states:

> An affirmative consent standard in the determination of whether consent was given by both parties to sexual activity. "Affirmative consent" means affirmative, conscious, and voluntary agreement to engage in sexual activity. It is the responsibility of each person involved in the sexual activity to ensure that he or she has the affir-

mative consent of the other or others to engage in the sexual activity. Lack of protest or resistance does not mean consent, nor does silence mean consent. Affirmative consent must be ongoing throughout a sexual activity and can be revoked at any time. The existence of a dating relationship between the persons involved, or the fact of past sexual relations between them, should never by itself be assumed to be an indicator of consent.[19]

I take this very clear and detailed formulation as the model of what tends now to define legitimate sexual practice at the legal and administrative level. It is no coincidence that it was California, pioneer of sexual liberation and "peace and love", that first asserted this new desire to code and standardise sexual relations. I am not saying this is either progress or an aberration; I simply see this law as expressing the logical consequence of the recoding of human practices, following the disappearance of cultural self-evidence and thus of implicitly shared understandings. The law states that there can be no such thing as implicitly shared understandings, only the explicit can be shared. If this is true, sex cannot be understood in culture. There has yet to be any law on the status of feelings...

The second dimension, after coding, is the integration of sexuality into a normative system—do this, do not do that. Schools and universities have had to submit to the law where there was one, or to invent their own regulations. We need only peruse the regulations of different schools to see that the Californian logic is everywhere. To take one example among many, the Lake Tahoe Community College has published a regulation concerning consent in sexual relations, formulated as follows:

Yes Means Yes. Together we can make sure that when sex happens it is a positive experience for everyone involved. This positive experience is based upon consent, mutual agreement by both parties involved to every action that occurs along the way. Consent means both of you are ready and willing to share that moment and that both of you have control over what that moment will be like. In other words, both people have to say "Yes" and to continue to say "Yes" as the interactions continue—this is what healthy intimacy is all about.[20]

Young people are taught not only what they must not do (which is legitimate for a school), but crucially, what they must do, as though instinct had suddenly disappeared, or rather as though two people no longer shared a culture, in other words, implicit and unspoken understandings. The code is there to manage nature when there is no longer a culture.

So, it seems that expanding the reach of freedom also expands the reach of standards and injunctions. And what is left of freedom then?

The taxonomy of gender

As is only logical, disconnecting code from culture opens the way to code switching, since the code is no longer part of nature or culture and can thus be learned. This is a performative act: I am what the code indicates that I am. Code switching can be tactical, particularly for a set of people who are dominated or even despised and are trying to gain recognition, not for their authenticity, but on the contrary by flexibly adopting the codes of the dominant group. The term "code switching" is said to have been first used in the 1970s by black American scholars to describe their interactions and relationships with white people. It involved hiding one's true self and adopting behaviour assumed to be more acceptable to the dominant group, notably in dating: "The greater the perceived distance, cultural difference, or racial difference between the two people involved, the more code switching is likely to occur".[21]

However, a perfect and prophetic example of code switching can be found in Jean-Paul Sartre's play *Le Diable et le Bon Dieu*

(1951), in which the hero, Goetz von Berlichingen, decides for a bet to switch from the role of rough mercenary knight called on by the nobility to crush the peasant revolt to that of charismatic, pacifist leader of the peasant movement. He plays a new role by choice. This comes as no surprise for an existentialist hero; in Sartre's philosophy, "existence precedes essence" and culture is a matter of choice rather than fate. But Sartre tempers this freedom of choice in his description of a café waiter, who was no doubt serving him as he was writing a chapter of *Being and Nothingness*:

> Consider this café waiter. His movements are animated and intent, a bit too precise, a bit too quick; he approaches the customers with a bit too much animation; he leans forward a bit too attentively, his voice and his eyes expressing an interest in the customer's order that is a bit too solicitous. [...] He is playing, amusing himself. But what, then, is he playing at? One does not need to watch him for long to realize: he is playing at being a café waiter.[22]

Code switching is never far from bad faith, which hides the authentic self. But if everything is code, what can be authentic?

Here we are approaching two domains in which the relationship between code switching and authenticity poses a problem. I am not talking here about what authenticity is; I note that actors and analysts refer to authenticity and that is enough for me to take it seriously.

In the domain of sexuality, personal choice is now seen as governing both biological nature and culture. This turns sexual desire on its head: society constructed gender and now I construct my own gender. In the 1980s the aim was to require the dominant culture to recognise categories that it underestimated or stigmatised by throwing the stigma back at the culture, proudly asserting one's homosexuality and demanding that the society legitimise that identity, for example by calling for the right to marry. But starting from this initial opposition of homo and hetero, today we have seen an expansion of gender categories based on self-identification, in other words without reference to biological sex. The existence of mismatches between biological sex and sexual identity is nothing new, but it was in the decade following Judith Butler's book *Gender Trouble* (1990) that they began to give shape to a broad movement. Our concern here is primarily the development of an open taxonomy of chosen identities (the number of categories is not limited, leading to a list in which letters and numbers can be added *ad libitum*, so to speak: LGBTQIA2+). This goes much further than the simple recognition of homosexuality, which was eventually accepted by conservatives. The resistance of (often religious) conservatives to this form of sexual liberation no longer targets the opposition of homo and hetero (which remains binary), but the fluidity of identities and the impossibility of fixing them in stable categories. Many conservatives are resigned to accepting homosexuality as long as it is constructed around traditional values (fixed sexual identities, marriage), and thus fits into a familiar cultural framework. Yet they reject the "uprooting" of sexual identities, while practising their own form of code switching through conversion therapies, where a person can give up being homosexual by "playing" the score of heterosexuality, under the supervision of an instructor.

This uprooting is underway, symbolically if not statistically, with sometimes unintended consequences. One Israeli couple, a man and woman, are both transgender and want to have children (using a surrogate)—a double transgression that circles back to a form of normality.[23] The desire for a child always puts family back on the agenda. In the same way, transgender people want to be recognised as full members of the other sex, which amounts to reaffirming the binary division we were supposed to have left behind. However, where gender is concerned the dominant call is for fluidity.

As often in the matters under discussion here, there is a question concerning the sociological importance and statistical scale of the phenomena. A minor news event can make headlines and lead to interminable debates while being statistically insignificant. But it is precisely this symbolic impact that is of interest to us, because this is what is at stake in culture. It is striking to see the exponential (and in this instance statistical) rise in the number of young people who describe themselves using the new nomenclature LGBTQIA2+. A Gallup poll in the US found that "roughly 21% of Generation Z Americans who have reached adulthood—those born between 1997 and 2003—identify as LGBT. That is nearly double the proportion of millennials who do so, while the gap widens even further when compared with older generations."[24] Crucially, membership of these new categories is strong among young people, as shown by the wave of abuse addressed to JK Rowling when she stated her reticence about allowing transgender women to use women's toilets.[25] The transgender movement has primarily targeted TERFs (trans-exclusionary radical feminists), an older feminist movement that played a major role in the struggle to challenge traditional gender categories. What is at stake in this aggression and in the young generation's demand for punitive normativity? They say that they are acting in the name of the suffering inflicted on transgender people by their exclusion from feminine space. Suffering is the new argument of identity-based challenges, as we shall see in the case of race.

Is it possible to be transracial?

If we can choose our sex, and thus if biological markers cease to be meaningful, can we choose our race? Rachel Dolezal was the representative of the NAACP (National Association for the Advancement of Colored People) in Spokane, Washington; she is a graduate of Howard University, an institution traditionally the preserve of African Americans. She became guardian to her brother (who is black and had been adopted by her parents); she married an African American man and had children who were seen by American society as black; she taught part time at Eastern Washington University on the following courses: "The Black Woman's Struggle", "African and African American Art History", "African History", "African American Culture" and "Introduction to African Studies". She wore her hair in dreadlocks and had tanned skin. She reflected the codes of "blackness". So, she was regarded as black and presented herself as black. We need to understand that in the US, even though it no longer has legal status, a single drop of black blood is all it takes to be considered black, so many people whose skin is somewhat dark are classified as "black", which would not be the case in southern Europe.[26] In 2015 her brother revealed that she was born white (and blonde) into a white family. The result was a scandal. She was accused of being a "race-faker" and lost everything. She was fired from her job, thrown out of the NAACP, her husband divorced her and she had to pay back a number of grants and loans. She defended herself by saying that she was transracial as others are transsexual, that she had made a free choice to identify with black people, that race had even less biological foundation than sex and that she did not understand why "transraciality" was criminalised when "transsexuality" was accepted.[27] The argument did not convince. She was condemned on all sides, from the courts to the black associations, progressive movements and, of course, the conservative right. For the press she remains an "infamous 'race-faker'".[28]

How should we understand this apparent contradiction? In both cases a biological given (sex or skin colour) is challenged in the name of free choice, personal sensibility and experience. This given is thus "fluidified", abandoned and reconstructed (if necessary, by surgery or pigmentation techniques) in order to subject biology to identity as experienced and chosen, which is then "coded" by references and behaviours that are regarded as those of one's new identity (in a similar way to converts to a new religion). In theory, Rachel Dolezal (who took the Nigerian name Nkechi Amare Diallo following the scandal, as a transgender person chooses a first name of the other sex or a convert takes a name reflecting their new religion) was right: race and gender are social constructions to which one can oppose one's authentic self (she uses the terms "social construct" and "true self" in the interview cited below).

To understand, we have to look at the different arguments of those who condemn Rowling's refusal to regard transgender women as women and those who condemn Dolezal for wanting to be recognised as black. The former criticise Rowling for saying that "sex is real", the latter respond to Dolezal by saying that "race is real". But the main argument of the former, denouncing the "suffering" imposed on transgender people by Rowling, is also used by the latter. The central issue is the link between suffering and identity: both the refusal and the usurpation of an identity hurt those who claim it.

A black American author, Ijeoma Oluo, interviewed Dolezal.[29] She wrote,

> I wrote two pieces on Dolezal for two different websites, mostly focused not on her, but on the lack of understanding of black women's identity that was causing the conversation about Dolezal to become more and more painful for so many black women.

Oluo's criticism of Dolezal is that she does not understand the suffering that being black involves; when Dolezal speaks of herself as having experienced a kind of slavery, Oluo sees this as profoundly scornful of the true suffering of slaves and their descendants. Black identity is suffering. Dolezal is dealing in cultural appropriation, borrowing segments of an identity, bits of culture, and appropriating them while not understanding what lies at the heart of this identity, which is suffering. For her, being black is a narcissistic pleasure and not empathy for the fate of a human group.

In Rowling's approach of "sex is real" and the "race is real" critiques of Dolezal, the word "real" means different things. The suffering of transsexuals is an individual suffering that is not rooted in a collective history. Racialisation, on the other hand, goes beyond personal stories; it relates to history and the issue of domination. Here we are coming to another contested point of the new thought: racialisation.

For in reality, race is becoming fluid. American censuses have abandoned the black/white binary. People can identify as black and white or choose from a constantly evolving list of races and/ or ethnicities; the idea of mixed race is now accepted, and so on. Race is not recognised by the law; those who demand the end of affirmative action do so in the name of anti-racism (race should not be taken into account either positively or negatively). Yet racism remains more active than ever in the US, as it does in Europe, in police attitudes, discrimination in housing and employment, and so on. It is here that the concept of "racialisation" is meaningful, since it confirms that this is a social rather than a biological issue. Racism is no longer grounded in the existence of biological races and the inequalities between them, and has become a way of seeing that racialises a person. The problem with this otherwise justified concept is that it can "deracialise" by including criteria from other categories in the category "race".[30]

Oluo maintains that "race is real" because the choice can only be made in one direction:

> You can be extremely light-skinned and still be black, but you cannot be extremely or even moderately dark-skinned and be treated as

white—ever... no amount of visual change would provide Dolezal with the inherited trauma and socioeconomic disadvantage of racial oppression in this country [...] How is her racial fluidity anything more than a function of her privilege as a white person?

So reality is constituted by the way we are seen by others, and this way of seeing is also a product of history, of a past that is not gone. "Minorities" do exist, even if it is hard to define what the "majority" is since, as we have seen, majorities now perceive themselves as "minoritised". We are not dealing with "communities" united by language, religion or shared culture, but with groupings around a set of markers that are meaningful through interaction with the rest of the society. Hence the fixation on these markers, and the condemnation of cultural appropriation that reveals their fragile status.

Identity is now a matter of choice, on the part of individuals themselves, certainly, but also, and perhaps still more, the choice of others, through the way they see me, or the list of categories that exist in the identity market. Dolezal used a "code" of "blackness"; she said that she was seen as black by white people. But in her account of her interview with Dolezal, Oluo begins by saying, "I'm sitting across from Rachel Dolezal, and she looks... white. Not a little white, not racially ambiguous. Dolezal looks really, really white." Here is a form of cultural insecurity, where an identity is constructed from floating, endlessly reconfiguring markers. Each of the two people conversing in this interview sees the other as a woman seeking to dispossess her of her identity, which means, for one, the weight of a shared past, and for the other, her freedom. The only way forward from here is to argue, based on one's own suffering, for this identity to be enshrined as a norm, the primary aim of which is to regulate the way that others see. Hence the importance of calls for censorship and limits on the freedom of expression to better guarantee one's own freedom to be. This circularity is undoubtedly vicious.

CAN WE CHOOSE OUR SEX OR RACE?

The demand for recognition is made with violence, be it purely symbolic or real. But this violence is neither political nor revolutionary, since it is not grounded in any collective imaginary, any utopia, but in a desire to copyright oneself.

7

SUFFERING AND REPARATION

From revolution to human rights

That the dominated suffer is nothing new. A revolution is precisely a revolt by those who have suffered from domination and want to end their suffering by overturning the established order, with the idea that, in the long term, this fight amounts to freeing the whole human race. As the *Internationale* puts it: "Arise ye starvelings from your slumbers [...] No faith have we in prince or peer / Our own right hands the chains must shiver [...] And the last fight let us face / The Internationale unites the human race". In revolutions, events take their meaning from the future: the French Revolution is said to be good because it heralded a future that was better than the Ancien Regime. Except that we are no longer living in a revolutionary period. The current ebb, which dates from the end of the last century and arises broadly out of the critique of totalitarianism (Soviet among others), is reflected in both a reinterpretation of the past and a mutation in the forms of struggle. The past is judged in the light of morality (the Terror of the revolution is now seen as an evil in itself, rather than a contingent or necessary excess), while the atemporal defence of rightness trumps the justification of means by their end.[1] From the 1960s to the 1980s, the conquest of rights for the dominated gradually became the overarching slogan for mobilisation (we should also remember the precedent of Suffragette activism on both sides of the Atlantic in the early twentieth century). Revolt is only "right" if it respects what is "good", in this case human rights. The struggle for civil rights in the US during the 1960s is archetypal in this regard. Demonstrations, petitions, political mobilisation and a concrete programme for change (affirmative action and bussing) sought to advance the cause without integrating it into a more all-encompassing ideological programme (such as socialism), even if the political left was more open to demands of this kind than the right. Feminism and the movement for gay rights adopted this model into the late twentieth century. There was a call for equal rights (parity, same-sex marriage) and new laws were drawn up and passed by parliaments without challenging political regimes. Activism was focused on a group ("women", LGBT, black people) who saw their struggle in terms of an expansion of democracy, and thus sought and found allies and support from categories of people who became involved not by reason of their gender, race or sexuality, but out of commitment to shared political values (liberty, democracy, equality), in other words a shared political culture. Although there were "separatist" feminist or black movements in the USA (such as the Black Panthers) the stress in the 1970s was more on an inclusive and universalist approach (exemplified by the Civil Rights movement and by the Equal Rights Amendment).[2]

But today, not only is revolution no longer on the cards, the simple demand for civil equality has lost momentum. What has disappeared is an all-encompassing view of society as a shared political space. The demand is for reparation, and the demand for reparation assumes a transactional relationship with domination: instead of overturning the system because it is bad, the aim is to require the system to recognise that it is not "good". The UN defines transitional justice (which enables the shift from oppression to reconciliation) as "the full range of processes and mechanisms associated with a society's attempt to come to terms with a legacy of large-scale past abuses, in order to ensure accountability, serve justice and achieve reconciliation."[3]

The key word here is "reconciliation", not "revolution". The primary condition for reconciliation—recognition of the suffering of the dominated—should then lead to reparation, which may be material but is primarily symbolic. Postcolonial countries, former slave-owning societies, and churches that have oppressed, raped and exploited indigenous people, children and women, must all recognise their crimes and make reparations for them.

From human rights to the right of the "self"

What has also changed is the nature of the collectivity. This is now not so much a community projecting itself into the future as a collection of individuals looking back at their own past and that of their (colonised and enslaved) ancestors, or who have discovered a hitherto concealed marker of identity (such as a sexual category). These new communities function in the manner of subcultures, as described in Chapter 2: they recognise themselves as a group on the basis of a limited, but always open number of markers, where the one common element is suffering. The demand for reparation is addressed to the others in the name of their past and that of their ancestors (slave-owners). Rather than the acquisition of new legal or political rights, the aim is to obtain protection for one's identity, which is assumed to be a good in itself. Yet it is a fragile good, to which it is hard to give existence in a taxonomy of identities that falls apart and recombines in an endless improvisation. It is hard to construct a community when people are engaged in a race to find small differences (the prototype being the LGBT++++ construction). This is shown by Réjane Sénac, citing Aurore Foursy, president of Inter-LGBT:

> the defence of liberty and equality under the law for all human beings "must be supplemented by a recognition of the specific needs of individuals", since, for example, intersex people do not have the same rights as the cisgendered whose sense of gender identity reflects the sex they were assigned at birth. According to Senac, it is thus fundamental not to seek "simple equality" but to recognise and respect the dignity of each individual according to their specificity and singularity.[4]

The staging of one's own suffering and its instrumentalisation in identity bargaining—or what Brown terms "suffer-mongering"—tend to centre identity on the individual person.[5] This saps the bases of any real collective action, leading to depoliticisation, and lines up individual life stories to the detriment of an overarching shared narrative, which alone can generate culture. The human geography specialist Chi-Chi Shi presents a very good synthesis of the feminist critique of what I would call "suffering individualism":

> Because this language presents systemic injustice through its effects on individuals, I argue that it is driven by a moralising impulse that leads to the rejection of power. Instead of mobilising to build collective power, we are left with a politics of individual demands, coming from an atomised set of subjective positions.[6]

Collectives are not or have ceased to be communities with their own culture that demand to be recognised as such. They are now constructions based on a set of criteria at once explicit and elusive (for example, what makes a person black? The answer is no longer evident). If identity needs to be defined in this way, it is no longer a fact that is felt and has meaning in a culture, a society and a history. This is how, entirely logically, the deculturation of identities affects political cultures, which used to operate within a particular territory (usually a nation state or empire) and were the product of a long history and usually long conflicts. Political life requires a shared vision of the issues facing the *polis*, the life of the city or nation, even if it means people kill each other to gain power there. But a shared political culture no longer exists because the political space is no longer invested with the desire of citizens. It does not appear as the key space in which to advance causes; instead it appears increasingly provincial, due to the decline of the nation state, and cannot settle a debate taking place on the scale of globalisation.

The end of politics

This depoliticisation of struggles renders any utopia powerless. Utopia has been replaced by moral judgement and support for categorial causes. Trump's America is symptomatic of this, as are the two places of protest to which it gave rise: the street corner where a black man was killed by the police, and university campuses. But the Black Lives Matter and cancel culture activists are strangely absent from the arena of politics itself: the most vocal students of the 1960s left their campuses to demonstrate alongside black people and to encourage the disenfranchised to register to vote (as shown in Alan Parker's film *Mississippi Burning*, 1988); today they demand a safe space for themselves, to shelter them from violence at once physical (which is understandable) and, crucially, symbolic. But in so doing, they remove themselves from other struggles. The intersectionality so much discussed on campus is not the conjunction of struggles of oppressed groups, but the presence in a single person of many different predicates taken from different categories (race, class, gender). Every definition of a person seems to come down to a person with predicates ("a person with a uterus", "a person with a disability", etc.), thereby segmenting any collective into ever more restricted sub-groups until we are left with one person in their singular uniqueness. More and more doctoral students are researching their own group and regard their membership of it as the only criterion that legitimates their research. The problem then becomes the infinite splitting of criteria of belonging. Only a woman can work on women, only a black woman can work on black women, only a black lesbian woman can work on black lesbian women, but ultimately there will always be one irreducible gap: there is a subject who researches (the doctoral student) and an object of study. I have found this interrogation in recent theses, clearly demonstrating that identity is always open: it is not possible to copyright a group.[7] Knowledge is not fusional. Plus, this endless segmentation of identities breaks down any solidarity on a scale large enough to make things happen.

This flight into infinitesimal subdivisions ultimately exhausts any reference to reality. Integration into social life is no longer an aim to be attained through the efforts of individuals (such as activism), but the mutual adaptation of the society and the individual. Suffering comes from society and its way of seeing, and it is up to society to recognise the individual's identity (so that this recognition will end that suffering). In this sense identity, which is primarily experienced as suffering, is never negotiable. And you cannot do politics when some elements are non-negotiable.

The American philosopher Martha Nussbaum, herself very active in social struggles, discusses the observable depoliticisation of the new demands in criticising the position of Butler, the philosopher of gender:

> The great tragedy in the new feminist theory in America is the loss of a sense of public commitment... Butlerian feminism is in many ways easier than the old feminism. It tells scores of talented young women that they need not work on changing the law, or feeding the hungry, or assailing power through theory harnessed to material

politics. They can do politics in the safety of their campuses, remaining on the symbolic level, making subversive gestures at power through speech and gesture.[8]

As the philosopher Paul B Preciado observes, "Yesterday the site of struggle was the factory, today it is the body."[9]

The question is whether, faced with the conservative counter-offensive illustrated by the American Supreme Court's decision of June 2022 on abortion rights, a new coalition for civil rights can override this identity-based atomisation of struggles and attention focused on those just like us.

* * *

Up to this point there has been a clear gap between intellectual discourse and social reality. In France alone, the demonstrations by social movements—from the major strikes against pension reform under the Juppé government in 1995, which almost certainly saw two million people in the streets, to those of the Gilets Jaunes in 2018—almost never reflect (with the exception of the Manif Pour Tous) the supposed great civilisational debate on "wokeism", "cancel culture" and multiculturalism (with its burqa, burkini and halal bourguignon) that so excites the media, intellectuals, social networks and politicians. A pro-burkini action in a swimming pool involves a dozen people; the same number is enough to interrupt a play, a lesson or a conference. Demonstrations by "patriots" against Islamisation and opponents of Islamophobia are never attended by more than a few hundred activists. The supposedly woke actions usually happen in a few closed spaces (campuses, swimming pools, theatres) and crucially in the parallel universe of social networks. Political struggle has left the streets and moved to Twitter. What remains of sporadic violence in the streets (Gilets Jaunes, black blocs, violent suburban uprisings and all the revolts to come) qualifies as either riots or staged protests, but not insurrection. Also noticeable is the fact that the growing debate around "wokeism" in both the US and France has occurred to the detriment of voter participation. Now, rather than using elections as an opportunity to protest, people make their voices heard through symbolic actions such as dismantling statues and speaking out. Protesters refrain from challenging the form of the state or its institutions, focusing on specific spaces, as we have seen. They demonstrate by making themselves visible and speaking out, but only to each other, in the fusional mode of a protected group. Hence the proliferation of calls for safe spaces, groups that are not mixed in terms of race or gender and above all, though less visibly, online communities. This disconnect between the intellectual and media impact of an event and its real near-insignificance is particularly flagrant in the case of the performance of Aeschylus' play *The Suppliants* at the Sorbonne (another closed space) on 25 March 2019. Black activists interrupted the performance on the pretext that some of the actors were wearing black masks reminiscent of the "blackface" that was prevalent in the US in the time of segregation, which involves a white actor blacking up to look like a black person, at once ridiculing black people and confirming the impossibility of their appearing alongside white performers.[10] Here we have all the ingredients of deculturation: the decontextualisation of a monument of high culture (what Aeschylus wrote no longer had any relevance), the focus on a marker of identity (black mask) taken out of its own historical, sociological and cultural context (the critique of blackface is meaningful in the American context, far less so in the French context), anachronism, a black and white (as it were) moral judgement, and a reference to the suffering of a group as the justification for the censuring action. Dozens of articles about this incident appeared in the French media, lamenting the importation of cancel culture, but most of these articles, and particularly those that appeared three years after the event, struggled to find any examples of cancel culture in France other than the *Suppliants* affair.[11] The telling and retelling of this anecdote became a social phenomenon in itself, but one detached from any sociological reality (the "black" population in France seemed caught between massive indifference and puzzlement). By being highly symbolic in relation to intellectual and moral disquiet, the story ultimately took on more importance than social movements.

Morality as reparation

Revolts of the past are now viewed in a moral light, levelled and shorn of their eschatological meaning. History no longer has a direction and is without end or future. It is seen in a rear-view mirror tinted with morality, graduated from good to bad, just to unjust. Revolution has been replaced by what Daniel Bensaïd has termed the "moralism of revolt".[12]

This moralist vision of history is haunted by the question, which camp would whoever is speaking have been in? We are caught up in a race to be "holier than thou", tormented by the underlying worry: what would I have done back then? Historians working on anti-slavery campaigners or the Resistance against the Nazis did not ask themselves this question. Of course they might have sympathised with the cause of those they were studying, but they studied the "bad" as well, for example investigating the genealogy of antisemitism or Nazism. So they were required to emphasise the complexity of an event or the ambivalence of a protagonist. As an example, Woodrow Wilson, US President 1913–21 and great defender of the rights of peoples and international law at the negotiations for the Treaty of Versailles, was an inveterate racist who had fired black staff members from the federal administration. While this leads to a revision of the pure hagiography of Wilson as a hero of emancipation, it does not mean that he should be erased from history or that everything bearing his name should be renamed, as some antiracist move-ments now demand. Historical sequences such as the American War of Independence and the French "Code Noir" drawn up under Colbert to regulate slavery are now seen solely through the prism of a counter-factual morality: how can I position myself today as "white"? Or, how would I have positioned myself? Would I have been an abolitionist or pro-slavery? For a historian these are meaningless questions and manifestations of anachro-nism, that mortal sin of historical study. But the question is entirely moral: to what extent am I responsible for abuses com-mitted in the past? Clearly, this question has meaning and valid-ity. Many in the post-war generation felt guilty by (family or symbolic) lineage: what would I have done in the place of my Nazi or collaborator grandfather, who said nothing or even prof-ited from the system?[13] This question has its mirror image in another: if I am black, to what extent can I argue for debt, for the right to compensation? Another critique made by many young American "woke" black people involves asking, what are white people playing at in trying to be "holier than thou"? Holier than their ancestors? Or than everyone? These young black people are critical of virtue signalling, which involves endlessly condemning and censuring without engaging in political action.[14] They are not interested in reconciliation; they want justice.

These questions of guilt are all entirely legitimate. But they have an impact on our loss of a relationship to history, and thus on the vision we can have of culture.

From God's suffering to human suffering

The return of a morality of suffering, sin and reparation is not unconnected to a certain religious morality, but it is entirely secularised. For the flattening of the world is also the debasement of transcendence. The suffering of Christ's Passion is central to

Christianity. Its key feast was Easter until Victorian England, led by Dickens, invented Christmas, where people could at last have a little fun (eating and drinking as a family and receiving presents). Since then, Christmas has expanded in every direction, to the point where its reference to Christ has become superfluous and is replaced by (Happy) Holidays.

But what is to be done with God's suffering in a flattened world? The answer is to transfer it to humans, but believers are not keen on giving up divine transcendence. How can they be made to accept such a debasement of suffering?

Here we come to the debate around blasphemy. The secularised Western world seems to have rejected the criminalisation of blasphemy as outdated and obsolete. It managed to cling on in some laws (in the UK) but was no longer applied. The publication of Salman Rushdie's novel *The Satanic Verses* in 1989 made it once more a burning issue, since it led to violent demonstrations by Muslims and even a fatwa calling for the death of the book's author. Over thirty years later, in 2022, Rushdie suffered an almost certainly related attempt on his life that left him with permanent disabilities. The intervening period saw the caricatures of the Prophet in Denmark (2005), which were reproduced in different ways and led in France to the massacre of the staff of *Charlie Hebdo* and the murder of teacher Samuel Paty. In a more minor and peaceful mode, the Catholic Church joined forces with various protest campaigns and acts of vandalism targeting posters, performances and art works regarded as blasphemous, including Martin Scorsese's film *The Last Temptation of Christ* in 1988, the artist Andres Serrano's photograph *Piss Christ* in 1987, the play *Gólgota Picnic* written and directed by Rodrigo García in Madrid in January 2011 and the subversion of Leonardo da Vinci's painting of *The Last Supper* in a French clothing advertisement in 2005. In relation to the latter, Mgr Vingt-Trois, then Archbishop of Paris, defined blasphemy as "a pre-meditated attack on God".[15] But secular courts cannot adopt such a position. So the only usable argument to prevent blasphemy is one that, rather than highlighting God's suffering, focuses on that of believers who see their faith insulted or ridiculed. This suffering is unrelated to transcendence (whereas the flagellant penitent's suffering is addressed to God, at least before being staged in great processions of flagellants, which now feature on UNESCO's World Heritage list!). Now, suffering Christians have entered the category of identity groups calling for an end to their suffering (rather than its exaltation in penitence), hence the appearance of Christian identity groups that act within the same legal framework as antiracist groups. In France these include the Agrif (Alliance générale contre le racisme et pour le respect de l'identité française et chrétienne—General alliance against racism and for respect for French and Christian identity), founded in 1984.

So the courts try blasphemy cases without reference to God, but with regard to the suffering and emotion of those involved. Lawyers use the argument of "injured religious sensibilities".[16] Believers have fallen into line and advocate for an identity; they suffer like the rest, demand reparation and seek to copyright the symbols of their faith. This is the equivalent of the denunciation of cultural appropriation by racialised, indigenous and dominated groups.

These blasphemy cases have resulted in a paradox: far from rehabilitating religion in the public arena, protests by believers have accentuated the deculturation of religion. The suffering of believers has become secularised; it relates to their personal feelings, their intimate selves, rather than to the sacred. They suffer like the rest, like homosexuals, although the latter are a category that Catholics and Muslims cannot support. Thus in big demonstrations protesting against intolerance, we might find that Muslims have set out their stall next to one for lesbians or transgender people.

Yet protests against the use of religious elements in art have another consequence. This is the disappearance of a shared religious culture that also enables non-believers to express themselves through religious themes, whether respectfully or in caricature. "Don't touch religion" translates as "ignore religion" if you are not a believer. The painting of the Last Supper subverted by advertising was a great work of art by Leonardo da Vinci. In the eyes of the fundamentalists who denounced its use, this painting belongs to them, when in fact da Vinci was the prototype of the great humanist artist. If the court rules in favour of the believers, it grants them de facto exclusive property rights over a religious reference, which cannot then be read, painted or represented by those who see it as simply shared heritage, available to all. What then disappears is the very idea of a culture shared by believers and non-believers alike.

Why moralism and culture do not make good bedfellows

In March 2007, a German judge in a court in Frankfurt refused to grant an accelerated divorce to a woman of Moroccan heritage who was beaten by her husband, on the grounds that "in this cultural milieu it is not unusual for men to exercise a right of chastisement. The petitioner, who was born in Germany, should have expected this when she married the respondent, who was raised in Morocco."[17] This is a typical "multiculturalist" argument, but since we do not know what the judge's political opinions were, the views she expressed could come from a position on either the political right ("don't go in for a mixed marriage if you want to avoid problems") or the left (respect for immigrant cultures). Here we can note a similarity between "woke" ideas and the development of jurisprudence (which predates them): culture is no excuse and, in the case of patriarchy, Islam or colonialism, can even be an aggravating circumstance. Just as respect for cul-

THE CRISIS OF CULTURE

ture cannot justify female genital mutilation, so the deep cultural roots of racism in Europe in the nineteenth and twentieth centuries cannot serve as attenuating circumstances for the intellectuals and politicians of the time. Moralism is not the monopoly of woke thinking, far from it. We find it in contemporary secularism. The difference is that the former regards history as a terrain of repentance for the dominant, while the latter focuses on the present and calls for religious "reform", but this time from the "dominant" point of view (in this case secular and indeed atheist), which nevertheless reflects the same concern for a normative correction in the name of a moral imperative.

Cancel culture does not reject high culture in itself, but acceptance is conditional on the moral judgement applied to the artist. The fact that an author is a genius, a politician who saved the nation or a scientist who was a benefactor to all of humanity does not mean we can forget their racist, sexist or homophobic writings or deeds. As often happens, this debate is nothing new. It applied to Wagner and regularly returns in France in relation to Heidegger and Céline. But here, what could legitimately be a critique of the ideological functioning of high culture simply becomes the moral stigmatisation of the artist or author. There is a shift from content to author, from ideology to morality and from critique to censure. Culture no longer sits above society but is reducible to the authors of the works under consideration. It is not a canon that has gained autonomy but remains the work of an actual person. This personalisation of the work is necessary for it to be subject to moral judgement. It means that the cultural aspect in both senses of the term (anthropological: "it was the culture of the time", and academic: "Céline is a genius") cannot be used to counter the moral judgement. Culture disappears from the domain of morality and norms.

Moral judgement deculturalises because it rejects the "cultural excuse", whether it is used by the dominant or the dominated, in other words both when it permits exceptions to the norm in the name of the specificity of a dominated culture, and when it is used to disqualify the dominant morality on the grounds of its historical villainy (such as colonialism). For example, the dominant French society does not accept that practices such as the wearing of the Muslim headscarf, let alone female genital mutilation, can be validated in the name of respect for the culture of the dominated. The partisans of "hard" secularism do not claim that secularism as the expression of their own culture—in this case Western culture (which would pose the problem of Europe's Christian roots)—but as a gain made by the secular struggle against religion, and thus as a means of access to universality. Meanwhile, those who protest against this authoritarian secularism see the assertion of dissident cultural values primarily as a form of resistance to domination, rather than as the expression of the soul of a people or an anthropological culture. For them, identity is a form of resistance rather than a given. In other words, behind culturalist discourse (the values of freedom are Western, conservative values embody the resistance of the dominated), each side is in fact claiming a form of universality: liberalism on the one hand, resistance to domination on the other.

In this way, the cultural markers of protest are reformulated in terms that are paradoxically compatible with the dominant culture: the burkini and headscarf are a matter of "my body, my choice". A girl asserting her right to wear the headscarf does not say, "I'm obeying the tradition of my ancestors" but, "It's to avoid the alienating eyes of men, to assert my identity", and so on. Movements that denounce the neo-colonialism of the dominant culture paradoxically claim to be constructing a "culture-free" space, where the norms that underpin the critique are not subject to critiques of norms. They support cultural minorities not because the values of those cultures (such as wearing the headscarf) are good, but simply because these values are markers of revolt and a rejection of domination. They see resistance to domination as a universal value in itself, even if paradoxically this moral universalism is expressed through cultural specificities (wearing the headscarf, rejecting homosexuality) which, in the dominant culture, would be supported by the most conservative sections of society, in other words those who are most likely to align themselves with the colonial past (in Europe) or white supremacy (in the US). For example, in May 2022 Idrissa Gueye, a Senegalese player for the Paris-Saint-Germain football team (PSG), was accused of homophobia due to his refusal to wear the rainbow shirt of LGBT pride. One section of the African press defended him in the name of supposedly anti-homosexual "African values" (although he had said nothing on the subject), regarding the promotion of homosexuality as an element of neo-colonial domination. Yet the concept of homosexuality as it is used today is absent from traditional culture, which has other categories with which to understand a "third sex".[18]

Both those who support gay rights and those who reject them refer to a universal principle, which is no longer associated with a particular culture but with a categorical moral imperative as defined by Kant, in other words one that escapes any cultural determinism. It is the absoluteness and primacy of the norm that make it a deculturing element, for to speak of homosexuality either positively or negatively is to place oneself above the complexity and specificity of cultures that have all managed the diversity of sexual identities in their own way. To transform these fluctuating identities into legal objects (and thus also into legal subjects) is to universalise them and detach them from any cultural context. This is why saying that African culture is opposed to homosexuality is as meaningless as saying that South American evangelical culture, or the culture of Marseilles (a reference picked entirely at random, obviously) is opposed to homosexuality. When, in 1986, the Catholic Church's Congregation for the Doctrine of the Faith decreed: "Although the particular inclination of the homosexual person is not a sin, it is a more or less strong tendency ordered toward an intrinsic moral evil", this is not a cultural vision.[19] It is a moral norm that is above cultures, a decultured norm. The obsession with norms (abortion, women's dress) seen in contemporary fundamentalisms (evangelicalism, Salafism) is a consequence of their break with both contemporary culture and the notion of culture itself.

In this situation, where culture is in practice always a resistance to the principle of universality and never universal (since a universal culture would no longer be a culture in the anthropological sense, at least as long as there is no universal society), any reference to a system of universal values is deculturing by definition. And if a culture like the one we call "Western" seeks to claim universality, not only must it deculture other cultures but itself as well, to follow through on the universalisation of its own values. Yet this universalisation can be imposed only through authoritarian normativity, since by definition culturally shared self-evidence no longer exists. And there's the rub. Why does culturally shared self-evidence no longer exist? Because society has ceased to exist (or exists only in degraded form). To understand how the expansion of normativity relates to both the promotion of the narrative of desiring individuals and the complaints of suffering individuals (the flip side of that narrative), we must look to a key factor in social recomposition: neoliberalism. As I said in my introduction, neoliberalism is not the cause of the problem, but it is doubtless a good example of the "elective affinities" uniting the elements considered in this book and which raise a simple question: how can social connections be recreated in such an individualised world? The paradox is that neoliberalism, which is much more than the modern variant of capitalism, is remarkably successful in combining the libertarian paradigm of the desiring individual with the expansion of normative systems, since it posits itself as the best manager of suffering. But at what cost?

8

THE JOY OF NORMS

Neoliberalism assumes that every individual has no community ties, is at least theoretically autonomous and believes in the market. It seeks to attract desiring individuals; it wants them to like what they do, to push themselves and to seek fulfilment. The other side of this success story is that of the "losers", seen as responsible for their own failure. Individuals are regarded as free agents in their own lives and employees as self-entrepreneurs, regardless of the dependency that goes with their status. "Uberisation" is on the way to becoming the model both for work and for social relations as a whole.

An illusion of autonomy must be cultivated for uberisation to work. Individuals must be given value, placed at the centre of social relations; their self-image must be taken into account. But while they are allowed and indeed encouraged to choose for themselves, this is solely in domains that do not undermine their relationship to the "real" domination. So they can choose their gender and realise their fantasies; they are entitled to respect; and their identity becomes a subject of great solicitude, particularly given that the space in which it operates is precisely that of desocialisation, which leaves the way free for neoliberalism. Their imaginary emancipation leads them to consume the products of their alienation (this is Fordism revisited: workers were paid enough to be able to buy the cars they were making; today we free desire but make the desirers pay for the instruments of their pleasure). This trend affects every domain, and it is why activities and social functions that were once simply free must now be paid for (hitch-hiking has been replaced by carpooling apps, the confidant by the therapist).

The end of the private space and its commodification

The private and personal no longer exist. As Facebook founder Mark Zuckerberg puts it, privacy is no longer a social norm. "People have really gotten comfortable not only sharing more information and different kinds, but more openly and with more people, [...] That social norm is just something that has evolved over time."[1]

The disappearance of interiority (everything must be transparent and explicit) brings with it the commodification of the formerly personal. Illouz has provided a remarkable description of this in relation to sexuality:

> Sexuality has become a cultural platform for the consumption of solid, standardised goods (such as lingerie, Viagra and botox), goods associated with an experience (such as cafés, singles bars and nudist camps), and more intangible goods, such as therapeutic advice on how to improve sexual performance and skills.[2]

The relationship between a couple, which modernity and the secularisation of religions had gradually turned into a private matter, has been rendered central to economic and political socialisation. Demands for wages for doing housework came alongside evaluations of the "emotional overload" and "mental load" borne by women who work outside the home and also do domestic work. True, Marx had seen the family as reflecting social relationships, in a way that was non-political and unchosen, but today the commodification of personal life is no longer hidden; it is understood within the framework of neoliberalism. This commodification goes hand in hand with an expansion of normativity. While we can be glad that marital rape is now a recognised crime—or rather that the marital exception in relation to rape has now been removed—it is at the price of a judicialisation of the personal. Similarly, we are witnessing the contractualisation of personal relationships. In some countries, including the US, a contract signed by two partners is legally binding. People can go to court to have their emotional suffering recognised. In this sense, privacy is not the protection of private life, since private life no longer exists (as we saw with the critique of psychoanalysis and the Seal of Confession). It has been reduced to a set of rules that define the conditions in which the mind can be revealed (we no longer speak of the "soul", even though the word had long had a secular use in literature).

When big business adopts inclusive culture

As we have seen, terms such as empowerment and agency that are used by emancipation actors from oppressed groups do not necessarily challenge power structures, since business can easily accept the emergence of categories of hitherto dominated or marginalised people, in some cases to make a profit from them. Indeed the ideal of individual emancipation (it is up to each person to achieve personal fulfilment and to do their best) is entirely compatible with neoliberalism, which has no difficulty adopting new values and new gender categories. Both sides (employers and employees) share this "inclusive" culture of desiring individuals, self-fulfilment, autonomy and a kind of self-harmonisation of social relations.

This cultural mutation is particularly apparent in the US, where it has found political embodiment. Until the early 2000s, the Republican Party was both pro-business and an upholder of conservative values. This was the coalition that supported Reagan and George W. Bush. But with the Tea Party and Trump, the Republican base has become very uptight about values (conservative, obviously), while big business has adopted a "progressive" culture more in tune with its neoliberal turn. This is not only true of the tech giants that began as start-ups and became leading companies, run by ex-young boomers raised with Sixties values, but extends to formerly very conservative companies, typified by Disney World and its largest complex in Orlando, Florida. Until recently this was the archetypal entertainment destination for traditional American families; but then Disney took an "inclusive" turn (such as recognising LGBTQ+ employees). This led Florida's conservative governor and (former) Trump supporter Ron DeSantis, who is anti-abortion, anti-equal marriage and an advocate of Christian values as understood by southern evangelists, to go to war against Disney World, threatening to attack it by applying forms of pressure more generally associated with the political left (ending fiscal advantages).[3] But big business plays the inclusion card by design.[4] Disney's strategy should not be seen as purely commercial, since it had a lot to lose in its clash with the governor of Florida and could not be sure it would regain left-leaning visitors to replace those it was losing on the right. This was more about the congruence of economic neoliberalism with the new inclusive values, with no necessary connection to the potential profits or personal values of business leaders (moreover many local franchises refused to follow Disney, not out of commercial interest but due to the religious convictions of their local managers).[5]

The expansion of normativity

This cultural rift in the business world brings with it endless disputes that end up in court. Can an employee assert their own moral or religious convictions if they do not match those of the company? Can business owners turn clients away on grounds of sexual orientation in the name of their personal religious convictions? A famous case in the US (Masterpiece Cakeshop v. Colorado Civil Rights Commission) was decided by the Supreme Court in 2018 in favour of a cakeshop owner who had refused to make a wedding cake for a gay couple (but as often happens, the judge avoided making any statements on the underlying issue, confining the ruling to the particular circumstances: the baker was willing to make the cake, but not the two tie-wearing grooms in sugar posing on the top).[6]

While adopting a progressive posture, neoliberalism avoids any consideration of the structural reasons for discrimination (starting of course with racial discrimination). It makes individuals responsible for their actions, turning racism, sexism and discrimination more broadly into a moral problem caused by bad thoughts or individual drives, and which can thus be solved by the establishment of ethical rules (banning all "inappropriate" words and actions), promulgated and imposed by ethics committees and resulting in sanctions, always against individuals. What we have here is a system of accusation, confession and transaction. A case arises through a complaint, in both senses of the term (expression of suffering, call for prosecution). Thus we are seeing a turn towards jurisprudence in law, because everything is reduced to individual cases and particular situations. We know that a news item can give rise to a new law (such as, in France, the law promulgated under President Sarkozy that limits gatherings in the stairwells of apartment buildings, when such situations could be managed using a more general legal principle, such as public nuisance). The law in the English-speaking world is better suited to this evolution, since it starts from concrete cases rather than broad general principles, which explains why European law (and notably that of the European Court of Human Rights) has adopted a similar approach, leading to a bureaucratisation of the particular as part of a particularisation of norms.[7]

Neoliberalism claims to uphold the values of the "good life", from healthy food (including on school cafeteria menus) to tolerance and self-fulfilment (or rather the fulfilment of one's "potential") via cycling and yoga. But once the basic principles have been set out (usually on the homepage of the company or university, where there is much talk of excellence, inclusivity, respect, tolerance, well-being and so on), the next stage in the process is to deploy an extensive set of regulations, undertakings, disclosures and warnings, with pop-up messages encouraging us to click our acceptance of the terms and conditions, group ethics, or ways to get help and make a complaint, with telephone numbers to call if we have any doubts or problems.[8] Individuals are endlessly required to sign charters and undertakings; this includes anyone who applies for a grant or job, enrols on a postgraduate programme, applies for a residency permit or visa, books a room at the town hall in which to get married, or enrols their children at a school or on a summer camp. Neoliberalism brings with it a considerable expansion of systems of normativity and the bureaucracy that goes with them, in complete contradiction to the harmony promised when desires are directed towards personal fulfilment and tolerance for others.[9]

Here lies the paradox of neoliberal normativity: it unfolds in the name of tolerance and "good", it combats "prejudices" and ignorance, and thus consistently teams up with authoritarian pedagogy. From this perspective the root of all evil is not society, but those individuals who have not understood, who remain slaves to their impulses or to the old patriarchal culture. Such systematic individualisation makes it impossible to take any socially determining elements into account; everything is understood in terms of individuals making good or bad choices. To find work one need only "cross the street", as President Emmanuel Macron replied to a young man who told him that he could not find a job in his specialist field.[10]

Here we can see the loss of shared self-evidence in action: the new social relations implied by neoliberalism must be constantly negotiated and even imposed on those who have not understood, notably that it was for their own good. This can, of course, be done in different ways: it can be a (more or less gentle) nudge encouraging people to move in what they must see as the "right" direction, so that later they can be persuaded that they went there by choice. The "nudge" idea was invented by two American authors, lawyer Cass Sunstein and economist Richard Thaler.[11] The prime example, tried in the 1990s in the toilets of Amsterdam's Schipol airport, was an etching of a fake fly inside a urinal. It was noticed that men took better aim and were less likely to splash on the floor, so cleaning costs were reduced. Other examples include footprints on the floor to encourage people to walk in the right direction, a seat belt that must be undone for a person to sit down (and that they thus do up again without thinking) and "conformist" information ("70% of people do this or that", with the implication, "why don't you?"). All these techniques are taken from behaviourism, the branch of psychology that studies "cognitive bias" without investigating individual "psyches" (we have seen that the refusal to consider the "interiority" of individuals, starting with the unconscious, was also part of the flattening of the world). But this method can only tinker round the edges; it cannot manage conflict and does not sanction.

The other, more direct pedagogical approach involves decreeing and imposing a normative code, assuming that any resistance can only be at an individual level; in other words, the time of collective revolt is past. Neoliberalism is also entirely at home with the new moralism. It followed the evolution from the conservative moral discourse of the 1970s—well described by James Hunter (blame falls on those who receive assistance, who do not work, while promoting the value of work and the family)—to a post-1968 moralism more focused on the individual.[12] The values have changed, but not the moralising approach to human behaviour, which is no longer the preserve of conservatives. A section of the political left has converged with right-wing individualist moralism, to the detriment of collective imaginaries and ideologies, proposing to end suffering through the moral redemption of the system. "Wokeism" is ultimately very Christian, and very much in step with the rest of western Christian culture.[13] The neo-reactionaries who attack wokeism reject the idea that the Christian west should repent its past, yet repentance is central to Christianity. Indeed, its constant self-criticism and attendant constant anxiety may have been one of the drivers of Western dynamism.

When neoliberalism adopted the values of self-fulfilment, group solidarity and social rootedness were systematically replaced by individualisation, with the simultaneous promotion of a discourse focused on values, which justifies the standardisation of deeds, words and individuals, in a context of normativity in both senses (defining a homogenous standard and imposing rules of behaviour). Like any other system of norms, this new variant is a means of control that renders individuals more vulnerable, since all individuals are liable to deviate—for example by doing or saying the wrong thing. This vulnerability affects both "the people" and "the elites". So the system is always open to modification and the potential repudiation of well-known and indeed popular personalities; it becomes almost arbitrary and unpredictable, no longer offering position advantages and leaving no one untouchable.[14]

THE JOY OF NORMS

Jorge Luis Borges took this logic of instability to the extreme in his story "The Lottery in Babylon", in which every action, decision and position is dictated by an endlessly repeated lottery, so that everything changes with every new draw.

In a society that is that fluid while also subject to meticulous normativity, how can culture develop?

Authoritarian pedagogy: can habitus be created?

Authoritarian pedagogy involves fostering and establishing new behaviours (*habitus*) in individuals by instilling into them a normative system that they do not see as in any way self-evident and may well run counter to their own inclinations. This normative system is supposed to promote "good" values. The underlying idea is that, through a mix of reproof and incentive, individuals will ultimately internalise these new values and a new culture will thus become established. This pedagogy is authoritarian because it rejects the validity of counter-discourse. For example, feminism will not hear any defence of an ideal of confident masculinity, while secularism cannot accept being countered by religious arguments. Authoritarian pedagogy thus assumes either an initial tabula rasa or the rejection of what was already there. So there is a negative perception of the (paternalist, neocolonialist, sectarian religious, etc.) culture to be countered, while the culture to be constructed does not yet exist. It is a project. So here we are on a terrain where culture has no positive aspect, since the old culture has been delegitimised and the new one does not meet the necessary condition of any culture, which is the presence of implicit, shared understandings.

We saw in Chapter 6 how educational institutions are implementing this kind of authoritarian pedagogy in relation to sexual life. It is present far beyond schools and campuses, in newspaper articles, radio programmes, changes to the internal rules of companies and institutions and the criminalisation of sexual harassment (and extension of the concept of harassment to other areas). The idea is to demasculinise the perception of sexuality by changing behaviours and representations, so that a new culture of sexuality emerges. The Canadian writer Michael Kaufman is within this pedagogical framework when he explains in his many public lectures and talks that:

> [my] intention is not to reprimand men, even if some things are of course reprehensible. It's the easiest thing to tell people what not to do.... So as a father we have to set an example by expressing some of our feelings, according to the child's age. We must also do half of the housework. And then there are some messages that must be passed on overtly. Boys will come home from school saying things about girls, homosexuals and so on, we have to help them leave these clichés and prejudices behind... In a way, there's no such thing as virility. It's a bit of a collective hallucination. It's not the same thing as biological sex.[15]

Ovidie, former porn actress, now a film director and author, also writes about the project of creating a new "grammar" (she does not say "culture", since what is under discussion is precisely a behavioural "code" rather than shared understanding): "How can we learn to desire sexual freedom? We need to create a new grammar, adopt a policy of experimentation."[16] In another interview she notes,

> The right thing would be to ask, regularly, if things are ok. 'Are you all right? Is it OK if I do this to you?' Those are some of the little things we could start doing without making it contractual and annoying. I think this could gradually become part of our culture and our practices. That's when it gets tricky: we are all going to have to get used to these little things, until they become automatic and we stop thinking about them. It's all these practices around the idea of consent that we could adopt, without having to sign contracts or create apps.[17]

This pedagogical approach, which is closer to a nudge, provides a very good description of what is at stake: how can we make a culture, in other words develop shared understandings? It's going to be tricky.

Because the pedagogical approach works only in part (or not yet), there is still the force of the law, as recalled in a poster campaign at the University of Geneva in 2019: "Your sexist jokes are so witty, original and hilariously funny I am going to tell them to my lawyer."

But this authoritarian pedagogy is certainly not the preserve of the progressive left. We can see it serving the opposite values in the conservative right. How can masculinity and sexual difference be rehabilitated? American evangelicals have started running courses in sexual reorientation for people with homosexual tendencies. In Europe such courses have often been prohibited by law, precisely because of the brutality of this kind of pedagogy. In both the US and France, groups are trying to organise "masculinity coaching" workshops, where men (the workshops are not mixed) relearn how to be confident as males.[18]

I am not saying that there is little to choose between these opponents and partisans of masculinist culture in terms of the values they uphold. I simply note that, though the former may be looking forward while the latter look back, they have two aspects in common: the feeling of being a minority threatened by the dominant culture and a recognition of the crisis in cultural representations of sexuality. They recognise that shared assumptions have disappeared and are seeking to reconstruct a common culture, however difficult that may be. If there is so much talk of "freeing speech", it is because we no longer share silence. What we have is dead silence.

* * *

Authoritarian pedagogy clearly affects every domain. It is also a form of punishment. Transgressors are required to attend awareness courses and even re-education. Reckless drivers are sentenced to carry stretchers for the emergency services, people who have committed a crime under the influence of drugs or alcohol are sentenced to go into rehab, violent partners are sent on courses to raise their awareness of domestic violence, sex offenders are required to have psychological monitoring, and so on.

Since 2015 the detox/rehab approach has expanded in Europe (though not in the US, where the punitive approach is dominant) into the terrain of terrorism and jihadism. Strangely, none of the violent radicalisms that Europe saw in the course of a very bloody century were treated under the aegis of deradicalisation. No legal system sought to deradicalise the anarchists, fascists, nationalists, separatists, leftists and others who committed acts of terrorism against civilians. So why jihadists? It might be said that this is a logical extension of the culture of authoritarian pedagogy in other domains. But why is there no deradicalisation programme in France for the extreme right, although groups of that persuasion are now also involved in terrorism? The only explanation is that Islamic radicalism is seen as grounded in religion, which justifies a different approach.[19]

In France this "religious" conception of Islamic radicalism has had the very particular effect of constructing secularism as a national "culture", implemented through authoritarian pedagogy. In 2018 the ministry of education began developing a campaign to impose secularism in educational establishments. This involves two pedagogical levels: teachers are trained by "trainers" and must then go on to train their students. We can call this authoritarian pedagogy because criticism of the content is not allowed. Indeed, several possible counter-arguments (notably based on the religious beliefs of students) are regarded by the law as potential crimes (under the vague headings of hate speech, arguments in favour of terrorism and various forms of discrimination). Ministerial circulars state:

All staff employed by the national education service are required in the course of their duties to exert increased vigilance in identifying students who are at risk of sectarianism. Should education staff suspect a risk of sectarian deviance, they are reminded that they must inform the head inspector or head of the educational establishment, who will then instigate assessment by a multi-category team (composition to reflect the issues), who will be able to discuss the indicators identified and to adopt an appropriate response.

The list of signals arousing suspicion include "Challenging parts of the curriculum or preventative action; Refusal to participate in outings or festive events organised by the school or establishment".[20] Aside from the very vague nature of these criteria, *laïcité* is entirely self-referential, since it refuses to see anything other than itself. There is talk of the "values of *laïcité*", but no one can say what they are, beyond repeating the mantra of tolerance, as shown by the ministry's poster campaign of autumn 2021, aimed at students. In this we read that *laïcité* is "Allowing Sacha and Neissa to be in the same pool", with an image showing a blond, blue-eyed boy (with a Slavic name in case the penny had not dropped) and an Arab-African girl with a non-specific name, together in a swimming pool. The word "religion" is never mentioned (nor is Islam). The result is that *laïcité* appears, at best, as a principle of cohabitation between ethnic groups, which is an entirely culturalist approach. For while the campaign covertly targets Islam, it defines Muslims as a racial group, which is farcical in the context of French secularism. At worst, *laïcité* becomes a hollow slogan. How can students be made to understand that this is about tolerance, given the refusal to hear (never mind listen to) any other discourse or critique, and when the addressees are young people facing forms of discrimination from the explicit (racial profiling) to the indirect (inexperienced teachers being sent to particular schools)?

Campaigns of this kind completely erase both the issue of religion (which cannot be avoided if we are dealing with *laïcité*) and the very notion of culture, since they promote a "way of life" on the model of the new European Commission that we cited earlier, but nothing like a "culture" (an educated Dominican friar might not wish to be in the same pool as Neissa, even if she were called Marie-Claire). Such campaigns promoting *laïcité* "code" social behaviours according to the single criterion of the visible markers of ethnicity. Deculturation, once again, is when we move from culture to codes and norms. Normativity does not take over when there is cultural domination, whatever form that may take, but because there is deculturation.

In the absence of "desirable" values, the only way forward is to create *habitus* through the repetition of actions and "instructions". This is what Elias called the "civilising process".[21] In his book he shows how a culture can be created through the implementation of explicit normative codes (primarily around the concept of "good manners"), which would seem to confirm the efficacy of authoritarian pedagogy in leading to a new culture once norms have been transformed into *habitus*. For example, spitting was once an accepted natural function, but the civilising process imposed a norm of not spitting, which ultimately became a *habitus* so that spitting arouses disgust and casts opprobrium on the spitter, without any need to put up signs saying "No Spitting. Offenders will be punishable by..."

But that is no way to make culture. Elias' thesis has been criticised because it was said to suppose an initial absence of culture.[22] But crucially, and as Elias himself showed, this normativity was linked to a process later described by Bourdieu, in the form of the construction of the symbolic space of "courtiers" and "good society", which was then able to impose norms through its "symbolic domination". These norms were thus largely dependent on a particular place and time, and on the sociological process by which a social class defined itself and set about reproducing itself around norms that it constantly strove to regard as an ideal for life, a system of values and a shared imaginary, in other words not simply a way of life reduced to the very lowest common denominators. A constructed imaginary of values, of good, gets in the way of authoritarian normativity, which is reductive by definition. The trainer can only criticise the bad attitude of trainees who do not allow themselves to be "civilised". This in turn gives rise to the figure of the "savage", the only proof that somewhere there must surely be a culture. Luckily for Robinson Crusoe, abandoned and alone on his island, he found a Friday (black, enslaved and naturally simple) so that he could go on thinking of himself as a man of culture by training a savage. The metaphor has not gone away.

CONCLUSION

HUMAN, NOT HUMAN ENOUGH

The trilogy of deculturation, coding and normativity seems now to structure all debates and strategies on every side, be they conservative, progressive, secular, religious, feminist, masculinist, populist, multiculturalist, sovereignist or globalist. Conservatives are nostalgic for a fake harmony of culture and identity that they themselves helped to undermine (at the times when they were in power in the US, France and the UK during the second half of the twentieth century, not only did they refrain from overturning liberal laws, but they often extended them); the multiculturalists and populists have reduced the very idea of culture to a set of markers with no real content; and religions have either become secularised or have turned into a litany of prohibitions. Both fundamentalisms and authoritarian secularism locate their norms in women's bodies (beards and head hair have never received equal treatment, which just goes to show that there are constants in the obsession with seemliness). Feminist campaigns are, for the moment, identified with the #MeToo movement, expressed in a demand for normativity in sexual relations, while anti-abortion movements are also on the rise and reducing women's bodies to a meticulous and bureaucratic tally of fertilisations and pregnancies. Whatever the values that motivated the pro-life activists, the implementation of anti-abortion policies is always first of all an instrument of control, devoid of all humanity and thus of life. The call for gender fluidity endlessly splits possibilities until it comes up against the unique, unclassifiable individual. Everywhere the law is asked to enshrine classifications chosen by individuals (binary for opponents of same-sex marriage or, conversely, an infinite reflection of the variations of desire) and the imposition of norms on a collection of individuals who no longer know how to be a society.

Challenges from cultural or postcolonial studies have involved deconstruction, but they have trouble offering positive definitions beyond suffering. So they become locked in a moralist tendency. Meanwhile—suffering being the most widely shared thing in the world—every individual has grounds for feeling they are part of a minority, including the populists who dream of an untraceable people who are to be found only in recrimination. We struggle to accept the possibility of a hierarchy of suffering. Pointing out that the vaccination campaign to counter Covid-19 bore no resemblance to Nazism is a waste of breath: my suffering is absolute, particularly if it is entirely in my mind.

Deculturation also produces derealisation, and is fuelled by it, to the point where the difference between real and virtual becomes hard to assert. War and massacres should be enough to bring reality back into people's lives. Yet, aside from those who suffer it (most often stunned by an event that always seems unthinkable), war is not so much ignored as denied. Particularly noteworthy in this regard is the extraordinary capacity of Russians not to want to know what is happening in Ukraine. We saw the same thing before with Holocaust denial, which has now expanded to cover realities that disturb any old certainties. Everything can be denied (the massacre of children at Sandy Hook school in Newtown, Connecticut, the moon landings, the deaths from Covid-19). Facts and evidence are discredited in advance. Donald Trump's spokesperson, challenged over her exaggerated estimate of the numbers present in the streets of Washington for the presidential inauguration in January 2017, said she was in possession of "alternative facts", in other words a different reality.[1] Yet such negationism is always countered with authoritarian pedagogy, punishment systems and repression that systematically miss their mark because they do not respond to the need for belief.

There are undoubtedly some good aspects to the current collapse of utopias, when we remember how murderous utopias can be. But it has brought with it a collapse of imaginaries, which have become refracted in the virtual world. Holograms do the living for us: avatars in the metaverse suffer sexual harassment and rape, as described by the first woman to tell such a story, Nina Jane Patel, who witnessed her avatar being sexually assaulted by two others. Is it reality or fiction, when the real and virtual worlds have merged into one and the suffering seems the same in both?[2]

Faced with this void, this derealisation, the terrain seems open to domination. Protests and challenges are imprisoned in individualism, closed spaces and a competitive victimhood that the theory of intersectionality cannot resolve. The insistence on suffering and all kinds of redemption and compensation means the issue of power is not addressed. Power itself remains invisible. The political arena is now no more than a theatre in which narcissistic actors perform for an ever older and sparser audience. With a few exceptions, the super-rich seem to have no ambition other than to turn the oceans into private bathtubs for yachts that they do not even use to amaze the little people, but simply to make their peers jealous. In this context the rise of conspiracy theories is easy to understand: there must be an order and a brain (or a group of brains) behind all this.

Foucault's model of governmentality seems to be turning into reality: order is established and can function because it has taken control of the private sphere.

If my intuition is correct, nothing now is private. The reason we are caught in expanding systems of explicit normativity is that the control of souls, minds, the unconscious, the ego and the self has stopped functioning. And this is not, or at least not yet, because individuals are rebelling, but because their private worlds have already been taken over and flattened by norms. There is no need for the clumsy mechanisms of propaganda foreseen by Orwell in *1984* and Huxley in *Brave New World*, or those established by the communist systems. There is no need to establish a means to govern souls, because we no longer believe in souls. Exhibitionism renders control of our private worlds unnecessary.

The traditional mechanisms for controlling the private and personal, which Foucault described so well (hospital, prison, church, school), no longer control anything at all. Far from rendering these mechanisms more effective, increased regulation and calls for trained behaviours and excellence empties them of any real efficacy because they lack humanity and have no end other than themselves. The authorities do not trust them. Wherever they can, they move to a higher level of repression that also uses the tools of the internet (as in China). In democracies they commission more and more investigations and surveys and keep consultants and think tanks in gainful employment. Experts are having a field day. Forecasters and futurologists have never had it so good, while being incapable of forecasting anything whatsoever. The political terrain is constantly shifting and heavy-handed systems of repression are very expensive, so politicians feel their way from one crisis to the next. The personalisation of power, which is evidently on the rise and evidently unstable, is the corollary of the crushing of institutions and intermediate bodies, as we have clearly seen illustrated in France since 2017.

CONCLUSION

Populism (a fantasy of a people mirrored by its leader) is the default political framework.

Yet revolt is possible precisely because there is nothing left to lose—not in terms of possessions, but of a private life to preserve. Everything is observed by others. In Orwell's *1984* the camera was everywhere. It still is, but today there is no one behind it, just statistics. We laugh at *Loft Story*, we are outraged by the exhibition of private lives in the trials of stars such as Johnny Depp and Amber Heard, we delight in the sordid details of the relationship between Monica Lewinsky and Bill Clinton. But what does that change, other than the lawyers' fees? The reason domination no longer works is that the norms have been adopted by everyone. Normativity is rife, but it is not imposed by governments. The good news is that it is up to people to take charge of their own lives.

The logic of "peers" is destructive, turning us into our own clones. To escape this logic, we must leave our protected spaces behind and rediscover heterogeneity, difference, and debate. There is a clear demand for sociability. Affinity communities are flourishing, but they are adding to the erasure of social connection. Beyond online and religious communities, we can see this in policies promoting "excellence" through the privatisation of education, which do not construct social classes so much as new categories of the privileged and new spaces where groups can be alone together. Conversely, things change when individuals seek to regain social connection in their real lives, in whatever remains of the social fabric. This is what gave the Gilets Jaunes their strength. People in deprived neighbourhoods and isolated villages sought to join forces and take action, not in the name of others that looked like them, but based on things that brought them together and the maintenance of community life. These forms of sociability remain very unstable and vulnerable unless they become political, in the sense of acquiring both political representation and a shared imaginary of what a society might be—beyond the simple promotion of a way of life through the infinite duplication of the everyday, and the reiteration of a few identity markers that have survived from a hypothetical culture of the good old days, golden age or glorious past.

How do we make culture? How do we reconstruct a social bond that is grounded in a shared imaginary? How do we rediscover being part of a community? Authoritarian pedagogy has never produced culture. At most it has generated a conformity of practices and indifference to values that have become simple mantras. Common to the normative systems of the kind described in this book is a deep distrust of human nature and human beings, even though the systems themselves are in part a product of the optimistic vision of the Sixties, in which desiring individuals achieve self-fulfilment through harmonious encounters with others. But the normative systems that are being established in the name of this freedom are dehumanising. They treat individuals as though they were infantile, selfish and incapable of understanding what is good for them, as they prey on the earth, on animals and each other. How are we to understand this contrast between the optimism of the premises and the pessimism of the conclusions? For as we have seen, what is now looming on the horizon is not utopia but apocalypse, of a variety for us to choose from our playlist of future worlds: global warming, civil war, the great replacement, a third (or fourth) world war, the return of the antichrist, epidemics far worse than those that have gone before, or simply old age and death. The care home is now central to debates on Western civilisation. Meanwhile, both deep ecology and antispeciesism merely acknowledge the real, imagined or even desired disappearance of human beings from a planet that has gone off course and is spinning out of control. What we are living through now is a true crisis of humanism.

NOTES

INTRODUCTION

1. "Emotional support peacock denied flight by United Airlines", nbcnews.com, 31 January 2018.
2. As we learn from the results of an IFOP survey of 15–17-year-olds conducted for LICRA (International League Against Racism and Anti-Semitism) and published on 3 March 2021.
3. Daniel Lindenberg, *Le Rappel à l'ordre. Enquête sur les nouveaux réactionnaires*, Paris, Seuil, 2002. A call to order was made (and still stands), but it was not the source of the new normativities.
4. Sketch "La politesse", https://www.youtube.com/watch?v=1FzmSf GDJ5Y. The same is true of Serge Gainsbourg: https://www.nouvelobs.com/culture/20210302.OBS40824/gainsbourg-cumulait-tous-les-vices-peut-on-encore-l-aimer-aujourd-hui.html.
5. Maureen Dowd, "Liberties; Leech Women in Love!", *The New York Times*, 19 May 1999.
6. Maureen Dowd, "Bill's Belated #MeToo Moment", *The New York Times*, 9 June 2018.

1. THE CRISIS IN QUESTION

1. The emblematic book in this regard is *The Camp of the Saints*, by Jean Raspail [1973], trans. Norman Shapiro, Social Contract Press, 1987. An interesting study on the view that the end of the world amounts to

the "world stopping" can be found in Jonathan Lear's book, *Radical Hope: Ethics in the Face of Cultural Devastation*, Cambridge (Mass.), Harvard University Press, 2008. Another classic of apocalyptic literature is Ernesto De Martino's *La fine del mondo. Contributo all'analisi delle apocalissi culturali*, Turin, Einaudi, 1977.

2. The Trilateral Commission, Bilderberg, World Economic Forum, George Soros' Open Society or the Council of Foreign Relations (all of which at least exist, unlike the Illuminati). A fine example of these imaginary connections can be found in Bat Ye'or's book *Eurabia* (Fairleigh Dickinson University Press, New Jersey, 2005) in which she explains that the European Commission deliberately opened Europe's doors to Arab immigration to please the Gulf states during the 1973 oil crisis (without realising that this migration had begun earlier at the behest of European industrialists in need of manpower and without seeing that the emirs in the Gulf have no sense of solidarity with the North African working classes).

3. The great classic in this regard is the highly critical book by Christopher Lasch, *The Culture of Narcissism. American Life in an Age of Diminishing Expectations*, New York, Norton, 1979.

4. Regarding France, see the opinion poll *La Position des Français(es) sur la PMA, la GPA et le don des gamètes* (IFOP, 2021). In the United States, only certain states imposed severe restrictions on abortion in the wake of the Trump presidency. The majority of public opinion disapproves of these measures. They were only made possible by the politics of Supreme Court nominations and not by a reversal of public opinion.

5. Kristin Kobes Du Mez, *Jesus and John Wayne: How White Evangelicals Corrupted a Faith and Fractured a Nation*, New York, Liveright Publishing Corporation, 2021.

6. James Davison Hunter, *Culture Wars: The Struggle to Control the Family, Art, Education, Law, and Politics in America*, New York, Basic Books, 1991.

7. Regarding this debate, see Olivier Roy, *Is Europe Christian?* [trans. Cynthia Schoch], London, Hurst, 2019; Pierre Manent, *La Loi naturelle et les droits de l'homme*, Paris, PUF, 2018.

8. "Élèves 'transgenres': Najat en a rêvé, Blanquer l'a fait," causeur.fr, 12 October 2021.

9. For Zemmour, see Michel Janva, "Éric Zemmour: 'le mariage homosexuel est une erreur et c'est à l'origine de toute la suite, mais il ne faut pas forcément rouvrir le sujet'," 21 October 2021, and "Éric Zemmour n'est pas provie," 24 October 2021, lesalonbeige.fr.

10. "Cheer Up, Liberals. You Have the America You Wanted." *The New York Times*, 2 October 2021. Ross Douthat refers to the Pew Institute survey: www.pewforum.org/2019/10/17/inusdeclineofchristianitycontinuesatrapidpace/.

11. The critique of the liberal illusion is naturally at the heart of Marxism. But more recently it has reappeared in other domains, for instance in the writings of the feminist Carole Pateman. Reiterating a common argument among conservatives (but of course from a different perspective), she suggests that the problem of the social contract is that individuals do not freely choose their communal bonds. These precede individuals in different forms (family, community, nation for conservatives, patriarchy for Pateman).

12. The case of Allan Bloom, who is rather a secularist "republican", also demonstrates the difficulty of maintaining the transcendence of knowledge and culture in the face of a demand to democratise this very culture.

13. Michel Janva expresses a traditionalist Catholic viewpoint: "The effort must begin well beforehand, and especially in the cultural realm, to make it understood that the values we embody are essential for all men. To do so, Gustave Thibon's thinking, for instance, is such a precious aid. He who affirmed that it is not up to a majority, whatever it may be, to decide what is true and good, but conversely, the point is to 'rally the majority of citizens to what is true and good.' Culture is also our everyday lifestyle, at work, in school, in the family where, through our witness, we must assert the need for a transcendence to escape materialism and individualism... Then true change can come about, the change that involves a renewed connection with the natural law that has been engraved in the heart of man and society since time immemorial by the Creator of all things" (lesalonbeige.fr, 12 May 2012).

14. See for example Michel Houellebecq's *Submission* (trans. Lorin Stein, Paris, William Heinemann, 2015) and Jean Rolin's *Les Événements*

(Paris, POL, 2015). Michaël Fœssel analysed this fascination for the apocalypse in his book *Après la fin du monde* (Paris, Seuil, 2012).

15. Concerning the economic aspect, see David Harvey, *A Brief History of Neoliberalism*, Oxford University Press, Kindle edition, p. 2: "Neoliberalism is in the first instance a theory of political economic practices that proposes that human well-being can best be advanced by liberating individual entrepreneurial freedoms and skills within an institutional framework characterized by strong private property rights, free markets, and free trade [...] if markets do not exist (in areas such as land, water, education, health care, social security, or environmental pollution) then they must be created, by state action if necessary."

16. Eva Illouz, *La Fin de l'amour*, Paris, Seuil, 2020, and *Les Marchandises émotionnelles. L'authenticité au temps du capitalisme*, Paris, Premier Parallèle, 2019.

17. This is the thesis developed by Béatrice Hibou in *The Bureaucratization of the World in the Neoliberal Era*. [trans. Andrew Brown], New York, Palgrave Macmillan, 2015, and David Graeber, *The Utopia of Rules: On Technology, Stupidity, and the Secret Joys of Bureaucracy*, Brooklyn, Melville House, 2015.

18. Bernard E. Harcourt, *Exposed: Desire and Disobedience in the Digital Age*, Cambridge, Harvard University Press, 2015, p. 99.

19. A situation Chi-Chi Shi sums up well here: "Simultaneously, the network structure of post-Fordist capitalism is one which effects the internalisation of control in employees, demanding continuous self-improvement as self-investment. The remaking of the subject as one of enterprise, the universal entrepreneur, seeks to collapse the distinction between capitalist and worker; between businessman and citizen. Workers are rebranded as 'human capital', and own themselves as assets, each responsible for their own worth. This is encapsulated in the concept of 'skill', which conflates the qualities of a person with their labour-power. Measures like the individualisation of workers' routines and the utilisation of performance-pay schemes on the part of employers attack the collectivism of unions that historically have improved collective conditions, and treat each individual worker as a sub-contractor" (Chi-Chi Shi, "Defining my own oppression. Neoliberalism and the demands of victimhood," *Historical Materialism*, 26 (2), 2018).

20. David Harvey, *A Brief History of Neoliberalism, op. cit.*, p. 23.

21. The Urban Dictionary (online) now defines bungabunga as an "erotic ritual which involves a powerful leader and several naked women." Information pointed out by *The Guardian*, 7 November 2010.

22. Daniel Cohen, *The Inglorious Years: The Collapse of the Industrial Order and the Rise of Digital Society* [trans. Jane Marie Todd], Princeton, Princeton University Press, 2021.

23. "Even though Facebook sells much of the information posted to it, it stridently maintains that all responsibility for fallout from the Facebook wall devolves entirely to the user. It forces the participant to construct a 'profile' from a limited repertoire of relatively stereotyped materials, challenging the person to somehow attract 'friends' by tweaking their offerings to stand out from the vast run of the mill" (Philip Mirowski, *Never Let a Serious Crisis Go to Waste*, New York, Verso Books, 2013, 112). Cited by Bernard E. Harcourt, *Exposed. op. cit.*

2. ANTHROPOLOGICAL CULTURE: THE ERASURE OF SHARED IMPLICIT UNDERSTANDINGS

1. Norbert Elias, in his book *The Civilizing Process* (1939) (first English edition by Basil Blackwell) posits a sort of "bottom rung" of culture in the medieval West as regards rules and manners. This approach has been criticised because it confuses the existence of rules (because in all societies, even in the West in medieval times, people's behaviour is never haphazard) and the explication of norms (in a discourse of "do this, don't do that" that in fact emerged at the end of the Middle Ages). But his book poses a good question: Why does a society at a given point in time feel the need to develop and impose an explicit system of norms?

2. Jonathan Lear, *Radical Hope: Ethics in the Face of Cultural Devastation*, Cambridge (Mass.), Harvard University Press, 2008.

3. Richard Hoggart, *The Uses of Literacy*, Penguin Books, Kindle edition, Chapter Two.

4. Laurent Bouvet, *L'Insécurité culturelle. Sortir du malaise identitaire français*, Paris, Fayard, 2015.

5. Monasphère is a real estate project that aims to bring together families

that share the same (Catholic) values close to a Christian church/chapel: https://monasphere.fr/.

6. Rod Dreher, *The Benedict Option: A Strategy for Christians in a Post-Christian Nation*, New York, Sentinel, 2017.

7. Rod Dreher, "Le projet Monasphère permettra aux chrétiens de vivre leur foi et d'en témoigner," FigaroVox, 20 January 2022.

8. One example among others on the Anti-Defamation League website: "White Supremacist Town Manager Envisions 'Homeland' for Whites," 22 January 2018.

9. Michel Lussault, *De la lutte des classes à la lutte des places*, Paris, Grasset, 2009.

10. Popular protests that took the names of colours or flowers: Revolution of Roses in Georgia, Orange Revolution in Ukraine, Revolution of Tulips in Kirghizstan, the Jeans Revolution in Belarus, the Cedar Revolution in Lebanon.

11. For instance, in Tunisia, prototype of the Arab Spring, where true freedom reigned for ten years, the post-2011 political and social sphere has remained vacant, except for networks formed under the former dictatorship, the Islamist party Ennahda and the UGTT (Union générale des travailleurs tunisiens—Tunisian General Labour Union), all dating from before the revolution. This void has been occupied by conservative political leaders such as President Kais Saied, elected in 2019.

12. Jean Raspail, *The Camp of the Saints* [1973], trans. Norman Shapiro, Social Contract Press, 1987; Michel Houellebecq, *Submission* (trans. Lorin Stein, Paris, William Heinemann, 2015); Jean Rolin, *Les Événements* (Paris, POL, 2015).

13. Richard Hoggart, *The Uses of Literacy*, Penguin Books, Kindle edition.

14. See for instance Philippe d'Iribarne, *La Logique de l'honneur*, Paris, Seuil, 1989.

15. Du Bois was not a multiculturalist. He did not glorify black culture and only used the term "culture" in the absolute, "culture" considered as civilisation: "The history of the American Negro is the history of this strife,—this longing to attain self-conscious manhood, to merge his double self into a better and truer self. In this merging he wishes neither of the older selves to be lost. He would not Africanize America,

for America has too much to teach the world and Africa. He would not bleach his Negro soul in a flood of white Americanism, for he knows that Negro blood has a message for the world. He simply wishes to make it possible for a man to be both a Negro and an American, without being cursed and spit upon by his fellows, without having the doors of Opportunity closed roughly in his face. This, then, is the end of his striving: to be a co-worker in the kingdom of culture, to escape both death and isolation, to husband and use his best powers and his latent genius." (W. E. B. Du Bois, *The Souls of Black Folk*, The Project Gutenberg (1996, updated 2021)).

16. Albert Memmi, *Portrait du colonisé*, 1957 [*The Colonizer and the Colonized* [trans. Howard Greenfield], London, The Orion Press, 1965].

17. Franz Fanon, *Les Damnés de la terre*, 1961 [*The Wretched of the Earth* [trans. Richard Philcox], New York, Grove Press, 2004].

18. André Burguière, *Bretons de Plozévet*, Paris, Flammarion, "Bibliothèque d'ethnologie historique," 1975.

19. There are also cases where a subculture decides to break away from the dominant culture, but in most instances, it ends up once again as a subculture of another dominant society: The Amish left Europe to wind up as a subculture in the United States; the society that the Mormons wanted to leave behind in their long trek westward ended up catching up with them.

20. JeanBaptiste Arrault, "Du toponyme au concept? Usages et significations du terme archipel en géographie et dans les sciences sociales," *L'Espace géographique*, 2005/4, t. 34; see also Jérôme Fourquet, *L'Archipel français. Naissance d'une nation multiple et divisée*, Paris, Seuil, 2019.

21. See Susan Neiman regarding the Peter Pan complex in *Why Grow Up? Subversive Thoughts for an Infantile Age*, Farrar, Straus & Giroux, 2015.

22. George Steiner, *In Bluebeard's Castle*, New Haven, Yale University Press, 1971, p. 118.

23. Allan Bloom, *The Closing of the American Mind*, Simon & Schuster, 1987, p. 68.

3. CULTURE AS CANON: THE FRAGILITY OF TRANSMISSION

1. "Every year, *Kunstkompass* ranks the list of the 100 most popular contemporary living artists, using a sum of scores reminiscent of Google's PageRank: it gives artists points for the shows they have had in such and such a museum, the museums themselves varying in prestige depending on the number of well-ranked artists they have promoted" (Dominique Cardon, *À quoi rêvent les algorithmes. Nos vies à l'heure des big data*, Paris, Seuil, 2015).

2. Readings, one of the most astute critics of the present institutional situation, sees a close connection between the crisis in higher education and the crisis of the nation-state: Bill Readings, *The University in Ruins*, Cambridge, Harvard University Press, 1997.

3. There are a few exceptions among universities with a "colonial" origin (American University of Beirut, American University of Cairo, Saint Joseph University in Lebanon) that were initially intended to provide the local elites with a "Western" culture. The late twentieth century witnessed the emergence of non-national universities (the European University Institute in Florence), and the conversion or transformation of long-standing universities into institutions with global ambitions (Sciences Po Paris, School of Oriental and African Studies in London, American University of Beirut and American University in Cairo), but this is in line with the general trend of globalisation and deterritorialisation that I study here.

4. Christopher Lasch, "Mass Culture Reconsidered," *Democracy*, October 1981.

5. The appearance of paperbacks in France in 1953 sparked a considerable increase in reading, but authors such as Henri Michaux and Julien Gracq would always refuse to be published in this crude format.

6. Another theory (Vladimir Propp for instance) explains why fairy tales circulate outside of their original context: it is because they reuse identical sequences that exist either in all cultures, or in the human subconscious (the child lost in the forest, the initiation quest, etc.). There is nothing contradictory about this, because structuralist theory and psychoanalysis alike seek precisely to go beyond culture, or—which in a way amounts to the same thing—to identify invariants that are at the

root of all culture, in other words basically a new "nature," human nature, which re-emerges each time culture takes a back seat.

7. Bill Readings, *The University in Ruins, op. cit.*, p. 87.

8. Allan Bloom, *The Closing of the American Mind: How Higher Education Has Failed Democracy and Impoverished the Souls of Today's Students*, Simon & Schuster, 1987, Kindle edition, p. 69. This is why the January 2022 announcement by the French education minister that the number of hours of Latin instruction would increase means nothing in terms of rehabilitating the classics.

9. *Ibid.*, p. 324.

10. Bloom's book is probably one of the most vibrant appeals in favour of classical humanist culture.

11. Christian Baechler, *La Trahison des élites allemandes, 1770–1945*, Paris, Passés/Composés, 2021. This remarkable book offers a clear demonstration of how Germany's intellectual and academic elite allowed itself to become intellectually fascinated by Nazism on the basis of its trajectory and not by constraint or some ecstatic "raptus" in 1933.

12. I entered a "classic" *lycée* (secondary school) in October 1960, following the Latin/German curriculum. But oddly enough, the start of Latin class was postponed that year in all French *lycées* to January 1961, and then, early in the following school year, it was pushed back an entire year, to begin only two years later. With hindsight, a measure that made no sense in itself was simply the cautious beginning of the marginalisation of Latin in secondary school. And this was under General de Gaulle, not under a "leftist" government. The advantages of learning Latin may of course be debatable, but it was the symbol of "disinterested" humanist culture and an educational tradition that was an end in itself.

13. Philippe Cibois, "L'enseignement du latin en France, une sociohistoire," https://cibois.pagespersoorange.fr/EnseignementLatinCibois.pdf.

14. "The other day I had fun—if you can call it fun—looking at the syllabus for the competitive exam for administrative officers. A sadist or a fool included in the syllabus questions about *La Princesse de Clèves*. I don't know if you have ever asked a postal clerk what she thought

about *La Princesse de Clèves*. Imagine the scene!" (excerpt from "Et Nicolas Sarkozy fit la fortune du roman de Mme de La Fayette," *Le Monde*, 29 March 2011).

15. An excellent summary of the question can be found in a short article by Thorsten Botz-Borstein, "A Religion of Excellence: About Administrative Fundamentalism," on Academia.edu.

16. On the origin of benchmarking, see Isabelle Bruno, "'Faire taire les incrédules'. Essai sur les figures du pouvoir bureaucratique à l'ère du benchmarking," in Béatrice Hibou, *La Bureaucratisation néolibérale*, Paris, La Découverte, 2013.

17. Philippe d'Iribarne's book emphasises the difficulty of importing foreign practices in the business world (*La Logique de l'honneur*, Paris, Seuil, 1989), but this same business world, by developing benchmarking, has decided to disregard the sociologist's advice and to demonstrate through practice that deculturation is possible.

18. A perfectly Huntingtonian book describes this precise case: Lawrence E. Harrison and Samuel Huntington, *Culture Matters: How Values Shape Human Progress*, New York, Basic Books, 2001.

19. An excellent description of how this happens can be found in Béatrice Hibou, *The Bureaucratization of the World in the Neoliberal Era*. [trans. Andrew Brown], New York, Palgrave Macmillan, 2015.

20. Cyril Taylor and Conor Ryan, *Excellence in Education: The Making of Great Schools*, London, Routledge, 2006. Note that Taylor was appointed to head Margaret Thatcher's think tank, the Centre for Policy Studies. He served as adviser to ten British secretaries of state for education (all of them Conservatives).

21. As the debate surrounding the scientific validity of anti-vaccine arguments put forth by both Professor Didier Raoult and the sociologist Laurent Mucchielli showed.

22. Dominique Cardon, *À quoi rêvent les algorithmes*, op. cit.

23. Sara Daniel, interview with Yoshua Bengio, "Les vrais dangers de l'intelligence artificielle," *L'Obs*, 7 November 2018.

24. André Fradin, "États-Unis: un algorithme qui prédit les récidives lèse les Noirs," *Rue89*, 21 November 2016.

25. Dominique Cardon, *À quoi rêvent les algorithmes*, op. cit.

26. *Ibid.*

27. The destruction of the mosque in Mosul and the pagan temples of Palmyra in Syria by ISIS come to mind, of course, as well as the fall of Timbuktu in 2013. I personally remember a magnificent mosque in Bargi Matal in the Afghan province of Nuristan made out of wood and using ornamental motifs specific to the local Kafiristan culture. It was destroyed by the Salafis in the early 1980s, deemed too closely associated with a pagan culture, and was replaced by a building made of concrete.

4. THE CRISIS OF IMAGINARIES

1. Michel de Certeau, "The Weakness of Believing," [1977] in *The Certeau Reader* [trans. Graham Ward], London, Blackwell, 2000.

2. According to Guillaume Le Blanc, "The reading of the history of societies over the long term that Certeau undertakes in his work shows that secularisation, in other words the transfer of the Catholic Church's objects/modes of faith to society, was coupled with a weakening of faith" ("La société des exodes," *Esprit*, January/February 2022, "L'amour des marges. Autour de Michel de Certeau").

3. In a video game such as *Karate & Sword Fighting Games* as well as in *Game of Thrones*.

4. See Thorsten Botz-Bornstein's analysis, *The New Aesthetics of Deculturation: Neoliberalism, Fundamentalism, and Kitsch*, Bloomsbury Academic, 2021.

5. David Graeber, *The Utopia of Rules: On Technology, Stupidity, and the Secret Joys of Bureaucracy*, Brooklyn, Melville House, 2015.

6. A similar *Fantasyland* is deployed among youth of all cultures: "science fiction has come to assemble a fairly standardized list of future inventions—from teleportation to warp drive—and to deploy them so regularly—not just in literature but in games, TV shows, comics, and similar material—such that pretty much any teenager in Canada, Norway, or Japan can be expected to know what they are." (David Graeber, *The Utopia of Rules, op. cit.*, p. 175).

7. André Malraux, *Le Musée imaginaire*, Paris, Gallimard, 1965.

8. James Clifford, *The Predicament of Culture*, (Cambridge, Harvard University Press, 1988), 1996, p. 121.

9. Jean During, "Pour une déconstruction des corpus musicaux canoniques d'Asie intérieure," *Anthropologie et Sociétés*, 38 (1), 2014.

10. For the history of lambada, see Leonardo García, "Le phénomène 'Lambada': globalisation et identité," https://journals.openedition. org/ nuevomundo/, 2006. Regarding the rhythmic cliché, *ibid.*, paragraph 42: "The lambada globalisation process took advantage of technical advances in synthesizers and beat boxes offering a variety of pre-programmed Latin 'patterns', which became widely accessible in the 1990s. Some of these instruments in their 'Latin' version, developed by Casio and Yamaha, include a wide array of Caribbean and Brazilian options that can be activated simply by pressing a button."

11. Nicolas Santolaria, interview with the semiologist François Jost, "A meme can serve just as well as a joke or to support propaganda for or protest against a sitting government," *M le magazine du Monde*, April 2022.

12. Via Lebanon: https://www.anissas.com/tempurasicilianstyle/.

13. "Furikake Masala is a successful combination of sesame and a typically Indian spice blend, garam masala. Two cultures meet and create a new culinary harmony" (https://www.limafood.com/fr/produit/furikake-masala).

14. Premiered at the Cannes Film Festival in 2004.

15. Example cited by Daniel Cohen, *The Inglorious Years: The Collapse of the Industrial Order and the Rise of Digital Society* [trans. Jane Marie Todd], Princeton, Princeton University Press, 2021, p. 129.

16. The unsurprising conclusion of the study: "More complex terminology increased perceptions of quality, likely choice, and pricing expectations." (Michael McCall and Ann Lynn, "The Effects of Restaurant Menu Item Descriptions on Perceptions of Quality, Price, and Purchase Intention," *Journal of Foodservice Business Research*, 11:4, 2008, p. 439–445, https://doi.org/10.1080/15378020802519850).

17. In Italy, it is the opposite: the doctor prescribes a *ricetta*.

18. Mario Vargas Llosa, *Notes on the Death of Culture: Essays on Spectacle and Society* [trans. John King], Faber & Faber, 2015.

19. Nelly Bowles, "God Is Dead. So Is the Office. These People Want to Save Both," *The New York Times*, 28 August 2020.

20. For a defence of the concept of religious acculturation (at odds with my view of deculturation), see "Pourquoi l'évangélisme est la nouvelle religion planétaire," interview with Sébastien Fath, www. mediapart. fr, 13 April 2021.

21. It would be worthwhile to do a study on the relationship between the local languages of Catholic (in particular Jesuit) missionaries and American Protestants. The former try to work with a written language, while the latter are interested only in the spoken word/oral exchanges. The White Fathers who specialised in North Africa read, write and speak literary Arabic as well as dialects. The evangelicals are only interested in *darija*, the local dialect (what I assert here is an empirical observation that requires verification). This sums up the difference between Catholic enculturation (adapting the Gospel to the local culture) and evangelical deculturation (purging the culture of paganism).

22. Like the grand finale of a fireworks display, "folklore" went through an unprecedented process of sophistication in the late nineteenth century: Breton headdresses became diversified and codified by region, music was recorded and transcribed by professionals, dialects were inventoried and classified; in Germany, museums of "local culture" developed in the late nineteenth century; see Véronique Charléty, *Itinéraire d'un musée, le Heimatmuseum*, Paris, L'Harmattan, 2005.

23. In both cases, the threat decried by progressives and ethnologists (after that posed by economic predators eager to burn down the forest) is the American evangelical missionary, a perfect example of deculturation without acculturation. In 1956, five American missionaries were killed by the Huaorani tribe in the Amazon, but a few years later their widows returned to the place and converted the tribe: there's no stopping progress. In November 2018, self-proclaimed missionary John Allen Chau was murdered as soon as he landed on a beach on the Andaman Islands; fortunately, he was single.

24. *Holy Ignorance* [trans. Ros Schwartz], Hurst & Co, 2010.

25. From what I glean from personal research, the term identity, which is on everyone's lips today, has only very recently undergone expansion in the social sciences. A quick glance at the titles of the *American Journal of Sociology* between 1950 and 2000 would seem to indicate

that the term at first only pertained to individual subjects (adolescents, for instance) and then in the 1960s, Black Americans and French Canadians, becoming more widespread as of the late 1970s.

26. James Clifford, *Returns: Becoming Indigenous in the Twenty-First Century*, Cambridge (Mass.), Harvard University Press, 2013. This book is essential reading to understand how vanished cultures are (re) constituted.

27. These examples are all taken from UNESCO's official list of Immaterial Cultural Heritage: https://ich.unesco.org/en/lists.

28. "Les falafels, c'est bien nous!" *L'Orient-Le Jour*, 18 March 2009.

29. See Éric Fassin, "L'appropriation culturelle, c'est lorsqu'un emprunt entre les cultures s'inscrit dans un contexte de domination," *Le Monde*, 24 August 2018.

30. Adam Forrest, "Jamie Oliver accused of cultural appropriation over 'punchy jerk rice,'" *The Independent*, 20 August 2018.

31. www.healthline.com/health/culturalappropriation#inpopculture.

32. "France Culture accuse l'écrivain Renaud Camus d'antisémitisme," *Le Temps*, 25 April 2000 (these passages were removed by the publisher from the original version published as *La Campagne de France. Journal 1994*, Paris, Fayard, 2000).

33. Pierre Nora (ed.), *Realms of Memory* [trans. A. Goldhammer], New York, Columbia University Press, 1996.

34. See Olivier Roy, *Is Europe Christian?* [trans. Cynthia Schoch], London, Hurst, 2019.

35. Especially the European Centre for Law and Justice (ECLJ), head-quartered in Strasbourg since 1998, which has the European Court of Human Rights and the European Parliament in its sights.

36. https://commissioners.ec.europa.eu/system/files/2022–11/president_von_der_leyens_mission_letter_to_margaritis_schinas.pdf.

37. *Ibid.*

38. Wendy Brown, *Regulating Aversion*, Princeton University Press, 2006.

39. Mahmood Mamdani, *Good Muslim, Bad Muslim: America, the Cold War, and the Roots of Terror*, New York, Pantheon, 2004.

40. Brown, *Regulating Aversion, op. cit.*

41. *Migrating to Flanders, Starterskit for family migrants*, published by the

Flemish Ministry for Civic Integration (Inburgering), with the support of the European Integration Fund, 2012.

5. COMMUNICATION: A MATTER OF CODES

1. Cited in Kelly Nix, *Intercultural Communication in Business: How Context and Other Cultural Factors Affect Communication in Multicultural Organizations*, CreateSpace Independent Publishing Platform, 2015.
2. Jean-Paul Nerrière, *Parlez globish. L'anglais planétaire du troisième millénaire*, Paris, Eyrolles, 2011. The examples I cite are taken from this book.
3. Spencer Hazel, "Why native English speakers fail to be understood in English—and lose out in global business", theconversation.com, 10 February 2016.
4. Domenico Cosmai, *The Language of Europe Multilingualism and Translation in the EU Institutions: Practice, Problems and Perspectives*, Éditions de l'université de Bruxelles, 2014, p. 86.
5. Kelly Nix, *Intercultural Communication in Business, op. cit.*
6. See Maurizio Ferraris, *T'es où? Ontologie du téléphone mobile*, Paris, Albin Michel, 2006. A mobile phone conversation begins with the recognition of the absence and unlocatability of the person we are talking to.
7. Dominique Cardon, *À quoi rêvent les algorithmes. Nos vies à l'heure des big data*, Paris, Seuil, 2015
8. "In recent years, the number of people diagnosed with autism has rocketed; a study of diagnosis trends, published in August, found the median age for diagnosis is 10 for males and 13 for females, and there was a 787% exponential increase in its recorded incidence, in the 20 years to 2018", Johanna Moorhead, "A lot fell into place: the adults who discovered they were autistic after their child was diagnosed", *The Guardian*, 16 December 2021.
9. Guillaume Paumier, "Ce que mon autisme m'a appris sur Wikipédia, Spock et les ordis", *Rue89*, 21 November 2016.
10. At the 2015 Wikimania convention Paumier gave a talk, "My life as an autistic Wikipedian". For a typical case of a person discovering their

autism and in particular how it "makes sense", see Annah Gadsby, "I've always been plagued by a sense that I was a little out of whack", *The Guardian*, 19 March 2022. The same thing can also happen to a family: Monia Gabaldo describes how she discovered that she, her husband and their three children were all autistic, in "Io, mio marito e i tre bimbi. Così abbiamo scoperto che siamo tutti autistic", *Corriere del Veneto*, 4 January 2022.

11. Élaine Hardiman-Taveau, president of Asperger Aide France, interviewed in the article "L'Entreprise et sa machine à café: l'enfer des autistes Asperger", *Rue89*, 14 May 2018.

12. https://en.wikipedia.org/wiki/Wikipedia:High-functioning_autism_and_Asperger's_editors.

13. Elena Giannoulis and Lukas R A Wilde (eds), *Emoticons, Kaomoji and Emoji*, London, Routledge, 2021. Giannoulis and Wilde take the example of the "Mister Hulk" emoji, which is supposed to express disgust, but does not in any way correspond to the "natural" expression of disgust. Yet the message still gets through, showing that the code is not a simple transcription of reality but remains a system that is arbitrary and thus symbolic.

14. We should remember that Leibniz saw Chinese characters as functioning through the logical combination of discrete elements, capable of expressing complex ideas in a way that could be instantly understood, since the character contained the definition of the word it expressed.

15. For an original approach, see Paul Dumouchel and Luisa Damiano, *Vivre avec les robots. Essai sur l'empathie artificielle*, Paris, Seuil, 2016. We should note that a Google engineer was suspended after saying that his chatbot had become sentient and could converse at the level of a seven- or eight-year-old child, notably concerning its fear of being disconnected. See "Google engineer put on leave after saying AI chatbot has become sentient", *The Guardian*, 12 June 2022. Either the engineer is prescient (artificial intelligence is taking the place of human beings) or Google is right (the engineer is mad), although the two options are not necessarily incompatible.

16. "Selfies en pleurs et 'sadfishing': quand les larmes se mettent en scène sur les réseaux sociaux", *Le Monde*, 7 April 2022.

17. Jean-Marie Bouissou, *Manga. Histoire et univers de la bande dessinée japonaise*, Arles, Philippe Picquier, 2010.

18. Giannoulis and Wilde (eds), *Emoticons, Kaomoji, and Emoji, op. cit.* Anecdotally, one day in Singapore my eight-year-old son wanted to buy the latest Japanese video game he had heard about. I took him to the shop and left him to explain himself to the seller. The game was just in, but the man said he only had the version in Japanese. My son wanted to buy it anyway so the man asked, "Do you speak Japanese?". My son answered, "No, but I play Japanese". The man refused to sell it to him—conscientious, but old school.

19. See the analysis of the Japanese messaging app LINE: Agnès Giard, "Emoji: les émotions sont-elles un langage?", blog on libération.fr, 13 May 2019.

20. Giannoulis and Wilde (eds), *Emoticons, Kaomoji, and Emoji, op. cit.*

21. On an older debate—since every period has its inexpiable crimes—see Gérard de Senneville, "Le secret de la confession: devait-on le violer dans le cas de lèse-majesté?" (written c. 1870, available on theologica. fr). His answer is no.

22. Catherine Meyer (ed.), *Le Livre noir de la psychanalyse*, Paris, Les Arènes, 2005.

23. Hervé Guillemain, *Extension du domaine psy*, Paris, PUF, "laviedesidées.fr" series, 2014.

24. Didier Fassin and Richard Rechtman, *L'Empire du traumatisme. Enquête sur la condition de victime*, Paris, Flammarion, 2007. We should recall that Freud, who had treated soldiers in a bad state of mental health during the First World War, rejected the hypothesis that adults could experience trauma caused by events.

25. Thorsten Botz-Bornstein, *The New Aesthetics of Deculturation: Neoliberalism, Fundamentalism, and Kitsch*, Bloomsbury Academic, 2021.

26. https://www.liberty.edu/behavioral-sciences/.

6. CAN WE CHOOSE OUR SEX OR RACE?

1. No culture has permitted rape in general, but each one strives to define what does and does not necessarily count as rape in the eyes of society

and the law, usually by transferring the blame to women (on the pretext, among others, of being provocative).

2. "1054 Strafanzeigen nach Übergriffen von Köln", *Die Welt*, 10 February 2016.

3. "Cologne: la police s'inquiète d'un nouveau phénomène, le 'taharrush gamea'", *Le Figaro*, 12 January 2016.

4. The events in Cologne were also analysed as a "male problem": "In conclusion, the events in Cologne show that, far from being an event linked to the presence of particularly misogynist refugees, sexual assaults and rape are part of a widely shared culture in which alcohol sometimes acts as a catalyst. So it is male domination as a whole that should be criticised here, not just the culture of other people" (Patrick Jean, "Agressions sexuelles de Cologne: un renversement révélateur", www.mediapart.fr, 14 April 2016).

5. Wendy Brown, *Regulating Aversion*, Princeton University Press, 2006, and Mahmood Mamdani, *Good Muslim, Bad Muslim: America, the Cold War, and the Roots of Terror*, New York, Pantheon, 2004.

6. Within a short period, the city of Nice experienced two attacks against people in a church: the first, perpetrated by a Muslim man on 29 October 2020, was automatically classified as an Islamist attack; the second, perpetrated by a non-Muslim on 24 April 2022, was regarded as a fit of madness. It is very possible that the qualification of the act was correct in each case, but it was immediate, before any investigation had been carried out.

7. According to the former housing minister under Nicolas Sarkozy, the things that these women were complaining about were nothing more than a pinch of machismo inherited from the "ribaldry" that "is part of French identity". She went on, "And I'm very fond of ribaldry" (*Valeurs actuelles*, 23 October 2017). We can also note the highly controversial petition signed by, among others, Catherine Deneuve, "We defend the freedom to pester, which is crucial to sexual freedom", *Le Monde*, 9 January 2018.

8. The Causeur site published a piece entitled "De l'art de la séduction halal" (29 April 2022), on sexual harassment in neighbourhoods populated by residents of immigrant origins, implying a correlation between religion and sexual harassment.

9. A Catholic website reflects the same culturalism. When Russian troops were committing gang rapes in Ukraine (which it did not mention), it posted a piece by Michel Janva which says: "Somalian immigrants attempted to enter a residence housing Ukranian women refugees, and terrorised them in their bedrooms. 'I was terrified. These things never happen in Ukraine.' In western Europe it has become normal. Welcome to our world... 'I was so scared I felt like going home'" (lesalonbeige. fr, 23 March 2022).

10. For a remarkable critical genealogy of the concept, see Carole Pateman, *The Sexual Contract*, Cambridge, Polity Press, 1988.

11. *Ibid.*

12. John Locke, *Two Treatises of Government*, 2nd ed., P. Laslett, Cambridge University Press, 1967, cited in Carole Pateman, *The Sexual Contract*, p. 52. Wiley. Kindle edition.

13. Nicole-Claude Mathieu, *L'Anatomie politique*, Donnemarie-Dontilly, Éditions iXe, 2013 (1st ed. 1991).

14. *Ibid.*, Chapter 2, "Homme-culture et femme-nature?"

15. Peggy Sastre: "the attraction to the worst criminals also relates to a female reproductive strategy" ("Pourquoi les pires criminels attirent autant", *Le Point*, 6 May 2022). The rather bizarre conclusion is that women choose men serving life sentences to enhance their reproductive chances!

16. Jean-Baptiste Pingault and Jacques Goldberg, "Stratégies reproductives, soin parental et lien parent-progéniture dans le monde animal", *Devenir*, 2008/3 (vol. 20). Other examples of this zoomorphism (or anthropomorphism, depending on the position adopted): "In recent years, many studies have shown the sophistication of mechanisms of decision-making in various species—and hence the deep biological roots of our political instincts" (Paul Seabright, "De la démocratie chez les chiens sauvages", *Le Monde*, 26 May 2018). On the dormant monkey within us, see "L'homme est un primate comme les autres: entretien avec Frans de Waal", *L'Obs*, 16 November 2018. On the fact that women are smaller than men (and that comes from monkeys): Peggy Sastre, "Si les femmes sont plus petites que les hommes, ce n'est pas à cause du steak", slate.fr, 22 December 2017. On the biological hypothesis of

homosexuality: "L'homosexualité est-elle biologique?", interview with Jacques Balthazart, *L'Obs*, 26 December 2013.

17. The details can be found in an article in *The Guardian*, "10 days in Sweden: the full allegations against Julian Assange", 17 December 2010.

18. "Dans le consentement amoureux et sexuel, il y a toujours une part de risque et d'inconnu", *Libération*, 10 April 2021.

19. https://leginfo.legislature.ca.gov/faces/billNavClient.xhtml?bill_id=201320140SB967.

20. https://www.ltcc.edu/campusresources/title_ix/yesmeansyes.php. (Emphasis original.)

21. Brianna Holt, "Do You Hide Your True Self?", *The New York Times*, 11 November 2021.

22. Jean-Paul Sartre, *Being and Nothingness*, translated by Sarah Richmond, Simon and Schuster, 2021, p. 102.

23. "She is a trans-woman, he is a trans-man, they are about to be parents together", *Haaretz*, 13 April 2021.

24. https://news.gallup.com/poll/389792/lgbt-identification-ticks-up.aspx.

25. "Harry Potter fans criticise JK Rowling after new 'transphobic' tweet: 'Please stop causing pain'", *The Independent*, 13 December 2021.

26. For once, I shall give a culturalist explanation. All the western colonial cultures were racist, but not in the same way: the Catholics (Spanish, French, Portuguese) constructed a range of variations between black and white: métisse, quarteron, mulatto, and so on. The Calvinists on the other hand (Afrikaners and American puritans), saw only black or white, and if you were a bit black ("one drop of blood") you were completely black. There is a clear parallel here with the theory of salvation. Catholicism established a transition between heaven and hell in the form of purgatory, whereas for the Calvinists, you were either damned or saved according to God's will; it is all or nothing, no nuances either with salvation or skin, no grey, only black and white.

27. "Rachel Dolezal: White woman who identifies as black calls for 'racial fluidity' to be accepted", *The Independent*, 27 March 2017.

28. A list of other race-fakers was provided by *Daily Mail Online*, 12 February 2021.

29. "The Heart of Whiteness: Ijeoma Oluo Interviews Rachel Dolezal, the White Woman Who Identifies as Black", thestranger.com, 19 April 2017. The following quotations are taken from this interview.

30. Juliette Galonnier's thesis, *Choosing Faith and Facing Race: Converting to Islam in France and the United States* (Sciences Po, Northwestern University, 2017) analyses the convert to Islam as "racialised" by conversion. As a member of the panel examining this excellent thesis, I challenged the term and would have preferred "ethnicised", since speaking of racialisation for a Breton convert to Islam seemed to me to empty the racial reference of the experience of people who are truly racialised. The convert remains profoundly white, as does Dolezal, which was the root of Oluo's criticisms of her.

7. SUFFERING AND REPARATION

1. This was François Furet's revisionist interpretation of the French Revolution and the whole anti-totalitarian critique from Claude Lefort and the journal *Esprit*, which delegitimised the "direction of history" with their rejection of the Soviet system and communism in general.

2. Of course this requires nuance; things did not happen in so linear and chronological a way. There was a black current in the US that from the outset was always highly sceptical of equal rights, leading to the "Nation of Islam" and the quest for absolute and asserted difference from white society. Similarly with the Black Lives Matter movement, many young black activists reject any link between reparation and a reconciliation in which they do not believe.

3. *Transitional Justice and Economic, Social and Cultural Rights*, HR/PUB/13/5, United Nations Publication, 2014, p. 5.

4. Réjane Sénac, *Radicales et fluides*, Paris, Presses de Sciences Po, 2021.

5. Wendy Brown and Janet Halley (eds), *Left Legalism/Left Critique*, Durham, Duke University Press, 2002.

6. Chi-Chi Shi, "La souffrance individuelle (et collective) est-elle un critère politique?", *Historical Materialism*, 26 (2), 2018. Quoted from the version in French, translation by Sophie Coudray and Selim Nadi.

7. See Diahara Traoré, reflecting on her own work, "Les théories coloniales

et leurs enjeux pour une anthropologie racisée: quelques éléments de réflexivité", in Naïma Hamrouni and Chantal Maillé (eds), *Le sujet du féminisme est-il blanc? Femmes racisées et recherches féministes*, Montreal, Éditions du Remue-Ménage, 2015.

8. Martha Nussbaum "The professor of Parody" *The New Republic* (Feb 1999).

9. Column in *Libération*, 20 July 2018.

10. The play's director, Philippe Brunet, has published a very interesting discussion of the affair, *Itinéraire d'un masque*, Lausanne, Favre, 2022.

11. Scuffles in the theatre seem to have been a French speciality since the disruption of a performance of Victor Hugo's play *Hernani* in 1830.

12. "Grandeurs et misères de Deleuze et Foucault", reprinted in Daniel Bensaïd, *Éloge de la politique profane*, Paris, Albin Michel, 2008.

13. Here is one banal example among many: Géraldine Schwarz, "What researching my family's Nazi history taught me about how to approach the past", *The Guardian*, 21 April 2021. She concludes: "I often asked myself: what I would have done under the Third Reich? I'll never know. But reading German historian Norbert Frei, I understood that the fact that we cannot know what we would have done 'does not mean that we do not know how we should have behaved'." Moral judgement is absolute; it knows neither context nor culture.

14. See the critique by the African American writer J Kameron Carter, "How a courtroom ritual of forgiveness absolves white America", *Religion News Service*, 4 October 2019, www.religionnews.com.

15. "Un spectacle caricatural par rapport au Christ", *Le Parisien*, 8 December 2011.

16. See Jeanne Favret-Saada, *Les Sensibilités religieuses blessées. Christianismes, blasphèmes et cinéma, 1965–1988*, Paris, Fayard, 2017. In 2005 the fashion designers Marithé and François Girbaud, who devised their brand's advertising campaign, were found guilty of an "insult" to Catholics. The poster parodied the Last Supper, replacing the apostles with scantily-clad young women (but the judgement was overturned by the Court of Appeal).

17. "Une juge allemande justifie la violence contre les femmes au nom du Coran", *Le Temps*, 26 March 2007. The judge was taken off the case.

18. See Coumba Kane's interview with the anthropologist Patrick Awondo, "Des qu'un Africain prend position sur l'homosexualité, l'affrontement symbolique avec le Nord se réveille", *Le Monde*, 29 May 2022.

19. Congregatio pro Doctrina Fedei, *Epistula de pastorali personarum homosexualium cura*, 1 October 1986, *AAS 79* (1987); official English translation available on the Vatican website: https://www.vatican.va/roman_curia/congregations/cfaith/documents/rc_con_cfaith_doc_198 61001_homosexual-persons_en.html.

8. THE JOY OF NORMS

1. Report on a speech by Mark Zuckerberg in *The Guardian*, 11 January 2010.

2. Eva Illouz, *La Fin de l'amour*, Paris, Seuil, 2020, and *Les Marchandises émotionnelles. L'authenticité au temps du capitalisme*, Paris, Premier Parallèle, 2019.

3. "Disney, Built on Fairy Tales and Fantasy, Confronts the Real World", *The New York Times*, 17 April 2022.

4. Tweet by the State Farm channel, 8 June 2021: "We believe no one should be afraid to celebrate who they are. Let's support our LGBTQ+ neighbors and show our Pride together! #GoodNeighbor #PrideMonth." Tweet by the Spanish branch of McDonald's, 23 January 2020: "McDonald's is proud to have a rating of 100 on the Human Rights Campaign Foundation's Corporate Equality Index, the national benchmarking tool on corporate practices related to LGBTQ employees." See also Mickaël Correia, "Le 'wokewashing', la nouvelle stratégie des majors pétrolières", mediapart.fr, 22 January 2022.

5. "Companies like State Farm and McDonald's say they support LGBT rights, but their franchisees and agents sometimes have other ideas", *Business Insider*, 23 June 2021.

6. See Winnifred Fallers Sullivan, "Is Masterpiece Cakeshop a church?" *Immanent Frame*, 8 June 2018.

7. Massimo Cuono, "Bureaucratiser l'inégal, l'extraordinaire, le particulier. Paternalisme et dépoliticisation à l'époque néolibérale", in Béatrice Hibou (ed.), *La Bureaucratisation néolibérale*, Paris, La Découverte, 2013.

8. In 2008 two professors at Carnegie Mellon university calculated that reading all the website privacy policies encountered by one person in one year would amount to 76 days of work. Cited in Shoshana Zuboff, *L'Âge du capitalisme de surveillance*, Honfleur, Zulma, 2018.

9. A bureaucracy very well studied by David Graeber, *The Utopia of Rules: On Technology, Stupidity, and the Secret Joys of Bureaucracy*, Brooklyn, Melville House, 2015; and by Béatrice Hibou, *The Bureaucratization of the World in the Neoliberal Era*. [trans. Andrew Brown], New York, Palgrave Macmillan, 2015.

10. *Le Figaro*, 16 September 2018.

11. Cass Sunstein and Richard Thaler, *Nudge: Improving Decisions about Health, Wealth, and Happiness*, New Haven, Yale UP, 2008.

12. James Davison Hunter, *Culture Wars: The Struggle to Control the Family, Art, Education, Law, and Politics in America*, New York, Basic Books, 1991.

13. In the American religious imaginary, the term "woke" suggests the great protestant "awakenings" scattered throughout North American history since the eighteenth century. For Americans the connection is clear. But in de-Christianised Europe, the Christian roots of "wokeness" are not felt and this leads to lamentations on the replacement of Christian culture by multiculturalism.

14. Of course there are still "winners". But the difficulty of putting names and faces to so fluid a system partly explains the popularity of conspiracy theories—there must be people behind all this who "understand" the system and are secretly manipulating it.

15. Interview by Marc-Olivier Bherer, "Nous assistons à une chose extraordinaire, la transformation de la paternité", *Le Monde*, 18 July 2018.

16. *Libération*, 28 July 2018.

17. Interview by Léa Mormin-Chauvac, *Libération*, 27 July 2018.

18. On a Catholic course of this kind in France, see the report by Jean-Marc Savoye with a punning title typical of *Libération* that is the despair of translators: "J'ai testé... plus de mâles que de bien", *Libération*, 20 July 2018. On the new trend of masculinity coaching, see the enquiry by the sociologist Mélanie Gourarier, *Alpha mâle. Séduire les femmes pour s'apprécier entre hommes*, Paris, Seuil, 2017.

19. I am not going to enter the debate on the nature of Islamic terrorism here, as I have dealt with it enough in other books (*Jihad and Death* [trans. Cynthia Schoch], London, Hurst, 2017). My concern here is the effect of policies founded on the premise of religious radicalisation, because whatever the validity of that theory, its effects are real.

20. https://eduscol.education.fr/980/prevention-et-lutte-contre-les-risques-de-derives-sectaires.

21. Norbert Elias, *The Civilizing Process* (1939) (first English edition by Basil Blackwell).

22. Étienne Anheim and Benoît Grevin, "Le procès du 'procès de civilisation'? Nudité et pudeur selon H P Duerr", *Revue d'histoire moderne & contemporaine*, 2001/1, no 48–1.

CONCLUSION: HUMAN, NOT HUMAN ENOUGH

1. *The Washington Post*, 22 January 2017.

2. Nina Jane Patel, "Reality or Fiction?" medium.com, 21 December 2021. In 2018, three students tried to publish bogus articles to mock the excesses of Critical Studies. One of these, entitled "Rubbing One Out: Defining Metasexual Violence of Objectification Through Nonconsensual Masturbation", concluded that masturbating while imagining a person without their consent was a sexual assault (Yascha Mounk, "What an Audacious Hoax Reveals About Academia", *The Atlantic*, 5 October 2018). This article was presented as a parody by its authors. In the metaverse it finds a kind of validation.

INDEX

INDEX

INDEX

INDEX

INDEX

INDEX

INDEX

INDEX

INDEX

INDEX

INDEX